SO-FMH-716

Author photo: Harold Levine

Front and back cover design:
Sarah Berman & Josh Walker for Cluny Sorbonne Media

Dove cover art: Tal

ISBN: 9798754552616

Contents

In honor of Tal's Bar Mitzvah

Acknowledgments

כִּי־פְשָׁעַי אֲנִי אֵדָע וְ-חַטָּאתִי נֶגְדִּי תָמִיד

For I recognize my transgressions, and am ever conscious of my sin.[1]

Learning something new can be exciting and empowering. It can also be a source of shame and embarrassment when you realize something that you should have already known. My first admission is that I am not particularly graceful. It doesn't come naturally to me. I'm aware enough to recognize grace in others and to know that I don't have it; while not knowing enough to achieve it myself. This space is frustrating, but it's what I have to work with.

For as long as I can remember, there have been kind folks, friends, and family who have tried to help me become better, for everyone's benefit. While I'm grateful for all of the conversations and care, I can't help but carry some disappointment and regret that I am only this far along.

---

[1] Psalms 51:5.

This is part of the messiness of the process: the more we learn about our contributions to the brokenness, the worse we should feel about the consequences of our complicity. I continue to find that one of the best ways to cope is to try to create change. When we take ownership of our actions and inactions, we are better able to transform ourselves and society.

Creating opportunities to learn more about how we impact others, without imposing the additional burden of asking others to make it easier for us by engaging in "teachable moments", is complicated. My holy friend, colleague, and teacher Rabbi Drew Alexander once told me "There's a reason why bats don't like to fly in Texas". I didn't know the reason, so he explained that since bats rely on echolocation to orient themselves, they prefer structures against which to bounce their waves. These are in short supply on the flat plains of Texas. We humans also need feedback to navigate where we are in relationship to others, and it takes special people to make that investment.

I've been guided by many amazing people along my journey who have contributed deeply to my sensitivity around gender. Professor Elizabeth Shanks Alexander and her husband, Reb Drew, have modeled a uniquely loving and supportive home.

My dear friends and teachers Seth Marnin and Rachel Tiven have patiently shared of their wisdom, counsel, and friendship. They also introduced me to my partner in life and living, Rabba Wendy Amsellem. She is the most graceful and gracious person I know. These traits somehow enable her brilliance, passion and limitless bandwidth for others to be compatible with me. For that gift, by the grace of God, I am eternally thankful.

These essays started with an article, co-authored with the amazing activist, leader, and thinker Rabbi Rachel Timoner for the Hadassah-Brandeis Institute. It then slowly evolved into a weekly essay for the incredible organization Bayit.

Being involved with the talented folks at Bayit is always a privilege and a pleasure. A very special thank you to the entire board, and its chair Rabbi David Markus, for all of the support and friendship. The process of converting an essay to a blog post, almost always on *erev shabbos*, was only achieved because of the loving skills and kind generosity of Rabbi Rachel Barenblat. You are an inspiration to all those who follow your teaching publicly as the Velveteen Rabbi, and an irreplaceable light to those who are fortunate enough to know you personally.

Congregation Beit Simchat Torah has been a home to me over the last three and a half years in innumerable ways. Beyond a platform and community, it has become family. Rabbi Sharon Kleinbaum, one of the great visionaries of our generation, created a position for me and in so doing demonstrated exceptional inclusivity and allyship. Her support and solidarity have made all of this possible. The clergy and administrative teams make the work a pleasant and holy offering.

While I write a lot, I still don't identify as a writer. It is important to me that what I am sharing is easily understood, even though at times streams of consciousness link the ideas together in my head and flow together. I come from a tradition where not feeling rigid boundaries to a particular topic is not only acceptable, but often valued. My apologies in advance if this style is less comfortable to read.[2]

Ellie Klibaner-Schiff has formatted and offered many helpful suggestions, enriching this book and making it better. The cover design is by Sarah Berman & Josh Walker for Cluny Sorbonne Media, incorporating artwork that my son Tal created.

I have been blessed to witness Tal's process of becoming a man, in his Jewish rite of passage. His soft and gentle thoughtfulness, paired with an internal strength of clarity and conviction, make him a model of graceful masculinity that continually inspires me. As much as this is written from a father to his son, it is mainly the lessons that he has taught me that are recorded here.

I've been so fortunate to have had the opportunity to study in Yeshiva and develop a love of learning from my teachers. They also gave me the gift of proximity to true greatness. Being on the receiving end of unbridled kindness and generosity has made it easy for me to recognize the goodness in people. I pray that this book finds favor with the Source of all Goodness and is a worthy reflection of my intention to try and get it right.

---

[2] I am often accused of writing in a stream of consciousness. That is because I often experience streams of consciousness and then I write them down.

Forward by Rabba Wendy Amsellem

המליך אות ת' בחן - ספר יצירה

God empowered the letter ת *within the word* חן. -Sefer Yetzirah

Brides and grooms embody a special kind of grace. They are loving and beloved, generous with their joy and full of wonder at the goodness bestowed upon them. But how does one maintain that grace on other days?

In our culture, masculinity is frequently problematized as toxic, overbearing, violent. Maleness can be seen as a syndrome in need of fixing. The project of this book is to explore a masculinity that is positive, generous, humble and loving; to make the grace of the bridegroom a quotidian experience.

The essays seek out elements of חן in each week's Torah portion and the connection of חן to the festivals of Rosh haShannah, Sukkot, Channukah, Purim, and Shavuot. חן is understood not as a superficial likeability or aesthetic but rather as an authentic commitment to speaking so that others will want to listen and constantly striving to fix the brokenness of our world. חֵן characterizes an ideal relationship with the Divine and with other human beings. Those imbued with true חֵן know themselves and are open to change, they are curious about others and fiercely determined to better society.

Graceful masculinity is a goal for all genders. It is a way of moving about the world with energy, conviction, and an easy humility. The fact that my bridegroom worked on this project during our first year of marriage is especially sweet for me as he understands that חֵן is a commitment to an ongoing project, rather than a settled state of being.

As we internalize the thoughtful messages of this book, may we merit to fulfill the verse[3] וּמְצָא חֵן וְשֵׂכֶל טוֹב בְּעֵינֵי אֱלֹהִים וְאָדָם

May we find grace and good counsel in the eyes of God and all people.

Wendy Amsellem
Elul 5781

---

[3] Proverbs 3:4.

Introduction

As much as I wish this book could exist independent of my identity and lived experiences, it can't. I am a straight, cisgender male with a very limited awareness of what is essential about gender. I hoped that my voice would be in the background, unnoticed, but it is the voice on the page.

This is not a book of theology about where gender lies or an exploration of God's pronouns. It is an offering born out of the struggles of simply being. These are my reflections on the difficulties of being a user-friendly human in the world. The challenges exist on a spectrum and are not person specific, as much as they are specific to being a person.

I understand God to be the source of all genders, and not limited by them. While talking about masculine attributes, God shouldn't skew to a masculine default. To the extent that it presents that way, it is due to the nature of the subject of masculinity, not the nature of God.

God has gender attributes and no body. We are created in the image of God - while acknowledging that God is imageless. I also believe that God gave the Torah on Mount Sinai to Moses and that it is infinite, eternal, and immutable. These are the truths that frame this book: Jewish tradition contains the insights to provide a healthy outlook on relationships, and we are all unique blends and reflections of the Divine.

The text that first inspired this project is a teaching from *Sefer Yetzirah*, the *Book of Creation*[1].

המליך אות ת' בחן וקשר לו כתר וצרפן זה בזה וצר בהם צדק בעולם יום שבת בשנה ופה בנפש זכר ונקבה:

[God] made the letter Tav king over grace and bound a crown to it, and combined one with another, and formed with them Jupiter in the universe, Shabbat in the year, and the mouth in the soul, male and female. (Sefer Yetzirah, the Book of Creation 4:14 Gra Version)

The חתן (groom/chasson) is a masculine archetype where a particular form of grace חן (*chein*) is governed and fuelled by the ת (tav) producing a model of graceful masculinity.

---

[1] Rabbi Aryeh Kaplan writes in the introduction to his translation that it "is without question the oldest and most mysterious of all Kabbalistic texts". Rav Saadia Gaon, in the tenth century, notes that according to tradition it is authored by the patriarch Abraham.

ת is the last letter in the Hebrew alphabet and represents
the wisdom of the Torah, a spectrum of conflicting forces,
and an acquisition of appropriate space.[2] My intention in
writing this book is to bring additional awareness,
language, and application of our tradition to the current
struggles around misused masculinity and to further the
exploration of gender based spiritual practice.

The rabbis have historically demonstrated tremendous
fluidity in applying gendered descriptions to people. For
example, we find the following story in the Talmud[3]:

כִּי אֲתָא רַב דִּימִי אָמַר הָכִי מְשׁרוּ קַמֵּי כַּלְּתָא בְּמַעְרְבָא לֹא כָּחַל
וְלֹא שָׂרָק וְלֹא פִּירְכּוּס וְיַעֲלַת חֵן כִּי סָמְכוּ רַבָּנַן לְרַבִּי זֵירָא שָׁרוּ
לֵיהּ הָכִי לָא כָּחַל וְלֹא שָׂרָק וְלֹא פִּירְכּוּס וְיַעֲלַת חֵן.

"When Rav Dimi came [from Israel to Babylonia] he said:
This is what they sing before brides in the West: No eye
shadow, and no rouge, and no braiding, and she radiates
grace. When the Sages ordained Rabbi Zeira, they sang to
him: No eye shadow, and no rouge, and no braiding, and
she radiates grace."

Rabbi Zeira doesn't identify as female and he isn't being
misgendered. The Talmud seems to be reinforcing the idea
that true grace comes from within and can't be self-applied
from the outside. It also isn't gender specific. By focusing
on particular character traits, a gendered component is

---

[2] See Graceful Inheritance.
[3] Bavli Ketubot 17a.

identified, elevated, and made accessible to people of all genders.

This is how I see the role of "groom" in this context. It is a very gendered quality but can be embodied by anybody.

These 58 essays, the numerical value[4] of the word חן, are intended to generate conversations, both internally and with others, about advancing the social dynamics of being. The dialectic component of this type of learning exercise is essential because facts here are less helpful than feedback. We often feel like we are getting it right until we are corrected by someone willing to invest in sharing their perspective, which then informs ours.

Learning Torah is no different. The first and last letters of the Written Torah allude to the necessity of learning together in a collective, as a prerequisite for proper comprehension.[5] The mouth, and using it to study the Oral Law, provides a unique opportunity to manifest

---

[4] Many of the essays here contain allusions to ideas that are concealed and housed through the Hebrew Alphabet. Gematria, a system of calculating the numerical value of Hebrew letters, is a rabbinic tool used to excavate deeper meaning in the text. They are not the sources of truths or teachings, but reflect them.
[5] Chamra Tava Page 2. The Torah concludes with the letter ל which means to learn when spelled out למד and begins with the letter ב, representing the minimum of two people to form a learning partnership.

grace. There are 524 chapters of Mishnah, corresponding to the value of the word חן when it is spelled out[6] חי"ת נו"ן.

In meeting and sharing in the world of ideas, may we merit to find more graceful ways of being together.

---

[6] 524 is also the numerical value of תלמוד בבלי - the Babylonian Talmud.

Sefer Bereishit

Bereishit - Graceful Beginnings

וְהָאָרֶץ, הָיְתָה תֹהוּ וָבֹהוּ, וְחֹשֶׁךְ, עַל-פְּנֵי תְהוֹם; וְרוּחַ אֱלֹקִים,
מְרַחֶפֶת עַל-פְּנֵי הַמָּיִם.

When the earth was bewildered and void, with darkness
over the surface of the deep, and the breath of God was
hovering upon the surface of the waters.

Genesis 1:2

From the broad admixture of chaos, and the simple order
of the Divine Spirit, comes the recurring opportunity to
establish a controlled structure to organize our world. In
an extreme example, the Talmud discusses how to advise
someone who is in a desert and loses track of time—to the
extent that they no longer can orient towards when *shabbos*
actually falls out.[1] Rav Huna posits that the individual
should recalibrate by counting six days from the present,

---

[1] Bavli Shabbat 69b.

and then observe *shabbos*. Chia Bar Rav argues the reverse: observe *shabbos* today, and then count six days.

The narrator of the Talmud opines that this dispute is predicated on whether we should look to the story of the six days of creation, or focus on the creation of Adam, to model the proper response to a breakdown in the system of arrangement. We find that the Code of Jewish Law[2] favors Rav Huna's position and rules definitively that one must first "create" for six days and only then can one sanctify a day of rest.

This of course begs the question: Why then, in the story of creation, is Adam only created on Friday, as opposed to on the following Sunday?[3] One of reasons that the Talmud[4] offers is "in order to enter into the *shabbos* immediately." This also requires an explanation because that isn't how the story goes; Adam and Eve found the time to eat from the forbidden tree on Friday before the sun set.

Menucha/rest isn't seen as the absence of work, but rather the completion of it. The *medrash* asks, "What did the world lack? Rest! Sabbath came—Rest came; and the work was thus finished and completed."[5] The "work" before the original sin is unrecognizable to what needs to be done now, to repair man's destruction of the world that God created. Adam mistakenly thought that the difficulty of just

---

[2] Shulchan Aruch 344:1.
[3] The Ohr Hachaim understand Shabbos to be in preparation for the following six days.
[4] Bavli Sanhedrin 38a.
[5] Genesis Rabbah 10:9.

being passive, and not sinning on Friday, and then entering into *shabbos*, was not enough to demonstrate his gratitude towards God. He therefore created more distance between himself and God, through disobeying God's instruction, and then needed to exert more effort to make up for it.

Adam ruined the perceived perfect to have a more relevant role in responding to the brokenness that he perpetrated. What he didn't appreciate, and what we are still suffering the consequences of, is that one can demonstrate agency through additional positivity, in response to goodness. That advancement of goodness is a healthy and holy act of creation that moves the world towards complete perfection.

The Rebbes[6] explain that Adam could have accepted *shabbos* early, and immediately entered it by adding from the week day to elevate the mundane to the holy. The mystics[7] explain that in that state of proactive completion, Adam would have been worthy to eat and delight in the previously forbidden fruit.

This principle and opportunity of adding onto the *shabbos*, known as *tosephes shabbos*, still pertains today,[8] and is alluded to in the first word of the Torah, בראשית, which can be rearranged to form ירא שבת—an awe/awareness of *shabbos*.[9] *Tosephes shabbos* is also represented in the final

---

[6] See Imrei Emes 689.

[7] Students of the Ariz"l.

[8] Shulchan Aruch 293:1 see also Ateres Zekeinim.

[9] See Sefat Emet in the name of the Zohar.

letter "*tav*/ת" of "שבת/*shabbos*," which has a foot, in the bottom left, that advances the holiness of the day further.[10]

We also find the letter "ת" governing over "חן/*chein*," grace, and corresponding to the *shabbos*.[11] Rest and grace are composed of the same two letters in Hebrew, and, like everything else in the world, their order makes a difference. The first time that a letter (or indeed anything at all) appears in the Torah, something abouts its core identity is revealed. The letter "*chet*/ח" is written in the Torah first as part of the word for "darkness"—חשך, and this alludes to the confusion that the evil inclination can bring to the clarity of our enlightened thoughts.[12] The *medrash*[13] frames this as a global struggle by teaching that "darkness," in this verse, is a placeholder for the Greeks in the Chanukah story, who wanted us to forget the Torah.

According to Sefer Yitzira,[14] the letter "ח," which is the eighth letter in the alphabet, is associated with seeing/awareness. That is one of the reasons that the *mitzvos* that have to do with seeing—i.e. the Chanukah candles and *Tzitzis*[15]—have eight days and eight strings.[16] Witnessing something isn't enough to effect change, but it provides an opportunity to create action. The letter "ח"

---

[10] Arvei Nachal.

[11] Sefer Yitzira 4:14 see introduction.

[12] Chamra Tava on Chanukah.

[13] Berashit Rabba 2:4.

[14] Chapter 5.

[15] Numbers 15:39.

[16] Chamra Tava.

itself forms a stationary door frame that then requires us to think about what movement is necessary in the moment.

Rabbi Naftali Zvi Horovitz explains that the intentional placement of this "ח" as the forty sixth letter (מ) in the Torah is because it forms the word for brain, מוח, and reflects its role in generating the thoughts that create the potential action of our bodies.[17] The letter "ח" is also the source of life, and when spelled out "חית" means life.[18]

The original human beings could have spent an eternity basking in the delight of a perfect world. Had we made it to the first *shabbat* without sin, we would have merited eating from the Tree of Life, and we could have experienced the ultimate pleasure of closeness to God. Because of our sin, there is confusion, void, and darkness; but also a customized part for us to play as an illuminating light of holiness. Before the original sin we could just add holiness, because that is what the world was lacking. Now we must constantly remember[19] the work of recreating the world that God originally envisioned for us, restoring the grace in humanity through a reorganization of the chaos into simple goodness.

---

[17] Zera Kodesh.
[18] Beis Aharon page 9.
[19] Sefas Emes Mekietz 640 forgetting is same letters as darkness in Hebrew.

Noach - Graceless Masculinity[1]

אֵלֶּה, תּוֹלְדֹת נֹחַ--נֹחַ אִישׁ צַדִּיק תָּמִים הָיָה, בְּדֹרֹתָיו: אֶת-הָאֱלֹהִים, הִתְהַלֶּךְ-נֹחַ.

These are the offspring of Noah: Noah was a righteous man, consistent in his generations; Noah walked with God.

Genesis 6:9

Noah's arc is long—he lived 950 years. Unfortunately, his arc bends away from grace. Parshat Bereishit concludes, and Parshat Noach opens, with Noah at his high point. He found favor in the eyes of God, he was a "righteous" man who "walked with God."[2] But just midway through the *parsha*, Noah tumbles from his exalted perch, becoming intoxicated and unclothed.[3]

---

[1] Originally published in a blog for the Hadassah-Brandeis Institute and co-authored with Seth Marnin.
[2] Genesis 6:8-9.
[3] Genesis 9:20.

Our rabbis teach that the 13 words in the first verse of Parshat Noach correspond to the age of bar mitzvah, the 13 years of becoming a man. By exploring Parshat Noach and examining how Noah fell from grace and righteousness, perhaps we can find insight into how to better advance lessons of positive and healthy masculinity.

The Hebrew word for grace, חן/*chein*, first appears in the Torah at the conclusion of Parshat Breishit when distinguishing Noah from the wickedness of his generation: "But Noah found grace in the eyes of *Hashem*."[4] It is not coincidental that the words "Noah" and "*chein*" are composed of the same two letters, "נ" and "ח," in opposite orders. This parallel foreshadows and teaches, in part, that Noah was going in the wrong direction.

Parshat Noach begins with, "These are the offspring of Noah: Noah was a righteous man, consistent in his generations; Noah walked with God."[5] This teaches us that the primary progeny of the righteous are their good actions. It was Noah's laudable behavior, particularly in contrast to the moral corruption of his time, that allowed him to find grace in the eyes of God. For the ten generations from Adam until Noah, no one acted in a way that was received gracefully by God. As long as Noah continued the work of refining his behavior, he was able to maintain this elevated position.

---

[4] Genesis 6:8.
[5] Genesis 6:9.

Here and throughout scripture, the verb "find" is associated with grace. Finding is a process of revealing that which was or is hidden. But unlike learning the whereabouts of a lost object, this is a relational "finding," where one learns they possess an attribute—in this case grace—in relation to another. It is a dynamic state or process rather than a finite or static state.

Noah's selfish pursuits continued when he emerged from the ark after the flood. He encountered a new world. Rather than check in to understand the environment, to see how he could make it better, he instead conducted himself in a selfish way. He provided for his own needs and followed his own desires. He planted grapes so that he could have wine, as opposed to something more beneficial for the world. Instead of making himself into a holy vessel of the Divine, he indulged in the void and debased himself.

This provides us with an opportunity to think about ways to become—and continue to be—righteous and graceful. It is essential that we learn to pay attention to and understand the world around us, to appreciate how our actions affect others, and to grow and evolve over time. We cannot presume to know how we impact others, because we are not the arbiters of how our actions are received. Instead we must constantly check in, listen, and modify our behaviors in response to what we learn.

It takes effort, humility, and a commitment to expand beyond the dismissive limits of "boys will be boys" to make real progress in the right direction. In our tradition, seven represents the natural order, and seven multiplied by itself, 49, speaks to the greatest expression of that exercise.

The spaces immediately beyond these points, 8 and 50, are transcendent shifts from the physical to the supernatural, like Chanukah and *brit milah* (circumcision after eight days), and the giving of the Torah, on the 50th day after the Exodus from Egypt. Fifty-eight is also the numerical value of Noah's name and of *chein*.

After Noah's failure, he doesn't throw himself back into the struggle for a more equitable world. He doesn't see his setbacks as an opportunity for growth or self-reflection. Noah learns no lessons, fails to grow, and falls from grace. Our rabbis teach that had he lived in the generation of Abraham, Noah would not be considered noteworthy. Indeed, Noah's and Abraham's lives overlapped for 58 years, but we hear nothing of Noah during that period. His name reminds us that when people of power and privilege fail to channel themselves for the betterment of humanity, when they fail to act as role models, they are not worthy of praise.

We read the story of Noah at the beginning of the new year, at the very beginning of the Torah, to remind ourselves of the human capacity to adapt and renew. It creates space to recognize the value and importance of understanding the ways in which our behavior impacts and influences others. As our world continues to evolve we must feel both empowered and responsible not only to construct our own new beginnings, but to never lose sight of how our words and deeds are experienced by others. We must affirmatively seek feedback and participate in that dynamic process in order for the arcs of our lives to bend forward and find grace.

Lech Lecha - Covenential Grace

וַיְהִי אַבְרָם, בֶּן-תִּשְׁעִים שָׁנָה וְתֵשַׁע שָׁנִים; וַיֵּרָא יְקוָק אֶל-אַבְרָם, וַיֹּאמֶר אֵלָיו אֲנִי-קֵל שַׁקַי–הִתְהַלֵּךְ לְפָנַי, וֶהְיֵה תָמִים.

When Abram was ninety-nine years old, Hashem appeared to Abram and said to him, "I am El Shaddai; walk before me and be perfect".

Genesis 17:1

God commands Abraham to be entirely perfect. It is difficult to perfect one's body and soul as the partnership between them is naturally contentious. The body is formed from the earth and the soul from Heaven; each yearns to return to its source. Without work, they will be in opposition to each other. This lack of harmony, according to the Sefas Emes,[1] is the deficiency that *brit milah*,

---

[1] Yehudah Aryeh Leib Alter (1847 – 1905) Poland.

circumcision, comes to fix.[2] Circumcision takes a site of physical desire, and consecrates it for spiritual purpose.

The commentators famously ask, "If Abraham kept the Torah, even though it had not yet been given on Mount Sinai, why did he wait to be commanded to be circumcised?"[3] One simple answer might be that circumcision is more than a physical act; it is the instantiation of covenant. You can't enter into such an intimate space—the space of covenant—without the consent of the other. Circumcision reminds us of the holiness of actions being determined by the will of another. Until God said "I want you," it couldn't be fulfilled.

For bodies to whom circumcision applies, circumcision allies the body to the soul which spiritually supports and enhances our actions. The temporary nature of the physical world gains permanence through a spiritual attachment. The Bris Kahunas Olam[4] observes an allusion to this in the verse "ימיו כצל עובר/His days are like a passing shadow."[5] In Hebrew, the phrase has a numerical value of 484, the same as body-soul/גוף נשמה. With the sixth letter vav/ו, the conjunction "and," the numerical value of this phrase "גוף ונשמה" equals 490 or תמים, perfect. The Zohar says the letter vav alludes to the site of

---

[2] Rashi shares an interpretation that this verse is referring to the commandment to be circumcised.

[3] Bavli Yoma 28a.

[4] Rabbi Itzchak Issac Katz (1550-1624) Prague.

[5] Psalms 144:4.

the *brit milah*.[6] When we use our bodies properly, we ensure that the soul is present and in partnership.

The early mystical work Sefer Yetzirah[7] writes that there are actually two covenants: a covenant of speech, and a covenant of circumcision. "When Abraham our father looked…God made a covenant between the ten fingers of his hands—this is the covenant of the tongue, and between the ten toes of his feet—this is the covenant of circumcision, and God bound the 22 letters of the Torah."

Ohr Tzvi makes a fascinating observation: the 22 letters of the Hebrew alphabet can map to the body! Starting with the toes of the right foot, those digits represent א-ה/*aleph-hey*. The next letter, *vav*/ו, is the "covenant between the toes" or the place of circumcision between the legs. If we continue to count the next five toes of the left foot, these are then aligned with ז-כ/*zayin-kaf*. The count then moves to the five fingers of the right hand, which correspond to ל-ע/*lamed-ayin*. The mouth, which is between the hands, correlates with the Hebrew letter פ/*pey*, which actually means mouth and represents the covenant of the tongue. We conclude with the five fingers of the left hand, and the final five letters צ-ת/*tzadik-taf*. All 22 letters of the Hebrew alphabet are represented on the body. This connects the covenant of the tongue with the covenant of circumcision.

---

[6] Halekach V'Halebuv '62.
[7] Sefer Yetzirah 6:7.

The Talmud[8] relates that right before Rebbe, the redactor of the Mishna, passed away, "he raised his ten fingers toward Heaven and said: Master of the Universe, it is revealed and known before You that I toiled with my ten fingers in the Torah, and I have not derived any benefit from the world even with my small finger." Reb Zadok HaKohen[9] explains this Gemara as a reference to being faithful to the covenant.[10]

The holiness of circumcision is dependent on speech. The numerical value of פה/mouth is equal to that of מילה/circumcision, 85. King David writes in Psalms, "grace/*chein* is poured onto your lips."[11] Perfection of speech requires mastering how to speak, when appropriate, but also mastering when to be silent.[12] Noah found grace and was called "perfect" in his generation. He is also praised for his use of sensitive speech.[13] However, he was deficient in that he didn't use language to help those around him improve themselves and be saved from the flood.

The Magid[14] points out that the measurements that the Torah gives for Noah's ark, 30, 300, and 50 cubits, spell לשן/speech or tongue—but the word is missing the ו/*vuv*.

---

[8] Bavli Ketubot 104a.
[9] Rabbi Zadok HaKohen Rabinowitz (Kreisburg, 1823 – Lublin, Poland, 1900).
[10] Takanas HaShavin.
[11] Psalms 45:3.
[12] Sefas Emes, Sukkot.
[13] Bavli Pesachim 3a.
[14] Dov Ber ben Avraham of Mezeritch D. 1772.

Noah did not connect to others through speech the way he should have, and in the end that manifested in the defilement of his body.[15]

Correctly using our mouth involves both putting words out into the world through speech, and silence in holding words back. This dynamic of expansion and containment is reflected in the two covenants. Rashi says that God's name *E-l Shaddai* is the name of God used in the passage about circumcision because there is ד'/*dai*/sufficient divinity for all. Yet the Talmud[16] relates that the *dai* in the name *E-l Shaddai* is also found in the context of God saying about the creation of the world: "that is enough." How can the same name of God refer both to God's relationship with the world as limitless, but also as contained?

Chein/grace is produced by expanding the holiness of our spiritual connections, elevating the mundane and each other, while minimizing the physical actions that could be in opposition with the spiritual. Pursuing perfection comes from increasing our awareness of the Divine Presence, and knowing that when we attach ourselves to God, we are made for each other.

---

[15] Genesis 9:21.
[16] Bavli Chagigah 12a.

Vayeira - Graceful Reflections

וַיֹּאמַר: אֲדֹנָי, אִם-נָא מָצָאתִי חֵן בְּעֵינֶיךָ—אַל-נָא תַעֲבֹר, מֵעַל עַבְדֶּךָ.

And he said, "My Lord, if I have found grace in your eyes, please do not pass from before your servant".

Genesis 18:3

Vayeira begins as Abraham, recovering from his recent circumcision, converses with God in a prophetic state. Suddenly, Abraham lifts up his eyes and sees three angels, presenting as men, approaching. He runs to greet them and then says, "My Lord, if I have found grace in your eyes, please do not pass from before your servant."

With whom is Abraham speaking? If he is speaking to the three men, why does he address them in the singular? Rashi offers two understandings of Abraham's words. First, Rashi suggests that Abraham is speaking to the three men, but he is addressing the most important of the three, and that is why he says "my lord." Then, Rashi shares an intriguing alternative approach. Abraham is actually speaking with God, asking God to wait while he goes to welcome the potential guests.

Based on this understanding of the verse, the Talmud teaches[1] that "Welcoming guests is greater than receiving the Divine Presence." But if Abraham is asking God not to pass on from him, why does he first run to the three men? Would it not make more sense to take his leave of God and then run to greet his guests? Also, how did Abraham know that it was acceptable to keep God waiting in order to service guests?

The Ramchal[2] frames[3] character development as an attempt to better understand God in order to act as God would act. "Walking in God's ways[4] - this includes all matters of uprightness and correction of character traits." He explains that this is what the Talmud[5] means when it teaches, "Just as God is full of grace and compassion, we should similarly be merciful and compassionate."[6]

The commentators[7] observe that the Talmud could have simply taught that we should be graceful and

---

[1] Bavli Shavuot 35b.

[2] Moshe Chaim Luzzatto (1707 -1746) Italy.

[3] Introduction to Path of the Just.

[4] Deuteronomy 28:9.

[5] Bavli Shabbat 133b.

[6] Rashi explains this teaching about grace, from Abba Shaul on the verse in Exodus of "זה א-לי ואנוהו", through the etymology ואנוהו = אני והוא, me and God—that we should make ourselves like God by doing as God does, adding to the *Braisa*'s understanding of אנוהו as the act of beautifying a mitzvah.

[7] בלבבי משכן אבנה.

compassionate because God is, but instead the Talmud links our actions to God's by making them conditional - to be God-like. In other words, the more we study and come to know God and the appropriate applications of God's attributes, the more similar we can be to God.

Abraham started his quest to understand God very early on, and now, 96 years later, he has perfected his body to be aligned with the Divine Will. R' Nosson Gestetner[8] writes that Abraham's 248 limbs were so attuned to their corresponding 248 positive commandments that his body naturally was performing in Godly ways.

As soon as his feet began to run towards the guests, Abraham assumed that was what God wanted him to do. Because God is charitable, Abraham knew that he was also meant to be charitable. Perhaps our verse should be understood as a question of approbation. After having left the prophetic state Abraham was asking, "If I have found grace in Your eyes, if I have understood You correctly, this is what You want me to do? If I have properly found Your way of gracefulness, please don't leave me because I am not leaving You." Abraham wasn't just walking in God's ways, but he was running!

Our relationship with God, however asymmetrical, is still reciprocal. Whatever Abraham did for his angelic guests himself, God performed directly for Abraham's descendants.[9] But whatever was done through a

<hr>

[8] (1932 - 2010) Bnei Brak, Israel.
[9] Bavi Bava Metzia 86b.

messenger, God also performed indirectly: *mida k'neged mida*, measure for measure. This principle can also be understood, homiletically, as reflecting God's *midos*, character traits. The more we understand God, the more we can be like God, and then the more God shares God's self in a relationship with us.

Perhaps the mitzvah of welcoming strangers is the example given here because one of the ways that we come to better understand God is by seeing different aspects of God in other people. It is now also a way to express to God, like Abraham did, that we come closer to God by treating people with kindness.

Chayei Sarah - Graceful Beauty

וַיִּהְיוּ חַיֵּי שָׂרָה, מֵאָה שָׁנָה וְעֶשְׂרִים שָׁנָה וְשֶׁבַע שָׁנִים–שְׁנֵי, חַיֵּי שָׂרָה.

The life of Sarah was one hundred years, and twenty years, and seven years, these were the years of Sarah's life.

Genesis 23:1

The *parsha* opens with the story of Sarah's death, but it begins with a description of her life. There are two unusual aspects to this verse, both of which have made it a particularly fruitful site for exegesis. First, there is the fact that the verse references the life of Sarah twice; at the beginning and end. Rashi explains that the repetition comes to praise her, and to teach us that the years of her life "were all equal for goodness." The first word, וַיִּהְיוּ, is a palindrome reflecting this teaching that, from beginning to end, and everything in between, Sarah's life was equally good. This is an unusual assertion as Sarah's life certainly had its ups and downs. After struggling with infertility for decades, miraculously having a son at 90 must have felt like a life changing experience for Sarah. The first word of the verse, having a numerical value of 37, also signifies this distinction by highlighting her 37 years of motherhood.

The Sefas Emes[1] writes that Sarah's days were all equally good because she was able to place God in front of her, always. Her clarity and awareness of God's presence was so real and consistent that it was powerful enough to heal the trauma of the original sin. R' Gedilah Schorr taught that this is alluded to in the verse "She bestows goodness, never evil, all the days of her life."[2] There was no mixture. Nothing impure.

Second, our verse also notes that Sarah was one hundred years, and twenty years, and seven years old, instead of saying more efficiently that she was one hundred and twenty-seven years old. Rashi comments that this alludes to the fact that when she was 20 years old she was like a seven year old with regard to beauty. Admittedly, this is a very strange compliment. What is the Torah trying to teach us in praising her in this way?

Sarah's beauty is lauded repeatedly in the Torah, prompting Abraham to fear that he would be killed by men who coveted her. The Talmud[3] explains that one of the reasons that Sarah was also called Yischah,[4] was because everyone wanted to gaze at her beauty.[5] Yet, despite her reputation for being exceptionally attractive,

---

[1] 656.
[2] Proverbs 31:12.
[3] Bavli Megillah 14a.
[4] Genesis 11:29.
[5] Another reason offered is that she saw with Divine Spirit.

the Midrash[6] claims that Abraham eulogized Sarah with the words from King Solomon's Woman of Valor[7] which include: "Grace/*chein* is false, and beauty meaningless, but a woman who is God fearing should be praised." Why is the Torah focusing on Sarah's beauty if, ultimately, beauty is not of true value?

The Torah is not singing Sarah's praises as much as it is praising her song. Whether high or low, she consistently connects to God. The rabbis observe[8] that the word for song, שיר/*shir*, is composed of the same letters as straight, ישר/*yashar*. Songs, like life, consist of changes. Wherever we are, we can respond by connecting straight to God. The Talmud[9] explains the verse in Psalms,[10] "I will sing of loving-kindness and justice; unto You, O Lord, will I sing praises," to mean: If it is loving-kindness, I will sing, and if it is justice, I will sing.

Sarah was exceptionally beautiful because she presented as the purest form of the divine image, like the natural holiness of a child. Expressing that connection constantly is what made her life good. When the physical is elevated, in service of heaven, then the physical is also praiseworthy, because it is being used as a tool for spirituality.

---

[6] Tanchuma 4.
[7] Proverbs 31:10.
[8] Sefas Emes 633 Beshalach.
[9] Bavli Brachos 60b.
[10] 101:1.

Rabbi Akiva teaches[11] that Esther merited to rule over 127 provinces of the Persian Empire because she was the descendant of Sarah, who lived 127 years. Sarah modeled an embodied revelation of the hidden that continues to give strength, especially in the hard times of exile and God's hiding.

Rabbi Tzvi Elimelech of Dinov[12] explains that Rebecca and Miriam also had this spiritual beauty that inspired people to connect more deeply to God. Unlike superficial beauty, true *chein*/grace produces a transcendent attraction that draws us closer to God, and to a deeper understanding of each other.

We read this *parsha* on the Shabbat that we bless the upcoming month of Kislev. In Hebrew, כסלו is understood as כס-לו, a covering for the 36 hidden lights of Chanukah, which we experience at the end of the month. Each month is connected to a different order of the four letters of God's name. Kislev's is organized[13] ויה-ה, the same as the last letters in the first four words of our initial verse, וַיִּהְיוּ חַיֵּי שָׂרָה, מֵאָה, and corresponding to the mourning of Jacob,[14] who was buried on Chanukah.[15]

---

[11] Bereishit Rabbah 58:3.
[12] Igra D'Kallah (1783-1841).
[13] Benei Yissascher.
[14] Genesis 50:11 וַיַּרְא יוֹשֵׁב הָאָרֶץ הַכְּנַעֲנִי.
[15] Emunas Asecha.

As we enter into the dark winter months, may the light of our connection to the Divine shine forth and bring true beauty to the world.

Toldot - Graceful Application

וְיַעֲקֹב נָתַן לְעֵשָׂו, לֶחֶם וּנְזִיד עֲדָשִׁים, וַיֹּאכַל וַיֵּשְׁתְּ, וַיָּקָם וַיֵּלַךְ;
וַיִּבֶז עֵשָׂו, אֶת-הַבְּכֹרָה.

Jacob then gave Esav bread and lentil stew; he ate and
drank, and he rose and went away. So Esav spurned the
birthright.

Genesis 25:34

Sometimes we just forget things. Often though, it's not
that we have actually forgotten, but rather that the clarity
of our knowledge is not sufficient to orchestrate our
actions.[1] If a person stays up most of the night playing
video games, it's not because they forgot that they have to
wake up in the morning for work. Rather, just knowing
that the alarm will ring soon is not sufficient to change
one's behavior.

עיין מתנת חלקו מ"י ד"ג השכחה אינו שולטת על הידיע, אלא על [1]
מה שהידיעה צריכה לגרום למעשה

When we say that remembering is a call to action, it is because we want to bring to the fore the knowledge that will cause us to behave appropriately. This requires an awareness of what we have "forgotten", so that we can counter the memory lapse and orient ourselves towards proper activity.

In our tradition, Esav had vast knowledge but there was a disconnect between what he knew and what he did; he was not a *talmid chacham*, a practitioner of wisdom. He would ask his father detailed questions about *halacha*, Jewish law, but he did not use that knowledge to influence his actions. Most egregiously, he was not self-aware enough to realize the tremendous gap between his education and his behavior. He thought he had nothing left to learn; the Hebrew words "Esav" and "complete" have the same numerical value.[2] He was completely unaware of how underdeveloped he really was. Our rabbis teach that this was the source of his evil and, like an undiagnosed illness, it never got treated.[3]

It is for this reason that Esav thought that he was fitting to receive the blessings of the first-born from his father. He didn't see himself as a sinner, and even the shock of rejection didn't arouse any introspection or change. Esav was "in his head," not connected to the rest of his body, or to the rest of the world.[4] Tradition teaches that Esav's

---

[2] ‏שלום = עשו = 376‏.

[3] ‏עיין נאות דשא אות ג‏.

[4] ‏עיין משנת רבי אהרן‏.

head is buried apart from his body, perhaps as a further expression of this disconnect.[5]

Jacob, by contrast, was constantly struggling, evolving, and throwing himself back into the fight for greater awareness. He was born at his brother's heel, thereby earning himself the name Jacob/Ya'akov (connected to the Hebrew word for heel, עקב/*ekev*). Jacob consistently fought his way up until God granted him a new name, ישראל/Israel, which is an anagram of לי ראש/*li rosh*, "you are to Me a head." With this name change, God gave Jacob confirmation of his holy transformation.

The space between intention and impact can be vast and even violent. How can we be expected to know what we don't know? Judaism teaches that knowing that we don't know is both a high level of knowledge and also a prerequisite for gaining greater wisdom.[6]

Acquiring this type of sensitivity is truly a gift that comes from the sensing of its absence. When we know that we are not there yet, that there is still much work to be done, then we can be open and worthy of receiving additional understanding.

We thank God for being our source of knowledge in the blessing "You graciously endow humans with wisdom," found in daily prayer. Wisdom is given with grace, and so being wise is not just about knowing facts, but knowing

---

[5] See Bavli Sotah 13a.
[6] Sefas Emes on Bavli Megillah 7b.

how to be with other people in a way that is graceful. This involves an awareness of how our actions resonate with others.

The Vilna Gaon comments on the verse[7] "You will find favor and goodly wisdom in the eyes of God and people" that "חן," favor, comes from the language of "חנם," free. It is for that reason, he posits, that "grace" is most commonly paired with the verb "find."

We can't rely on our subjective understanding of what's appropriate based on how we intend an action in our heads. Instead, we need to check in and hear from those being affected by what we do. Esav spurned his birthright by minimizing the consequences of his actions. In the mystical tradition, his ministering angel governs through the power of forgetting. Recognizing that wisdom comes from beyond us should humble us, and encourage us to take on the responsibility to internalize wisdom, commit to its application, and regularly review the space between the ideal and our lived, embodied experiences.

---

[7] Proverbs 3:4.

Vayeitzei - Graceful Growth

וַיַּעֲבֹד יַעֲקֹב בְּרָחֵל, שֶׁבַע שָׁנִים; וַיִּהְיוּ בְעֵינָיו כְּיָמִים אֲחָדִים,
בְּאַהֲבָתוֹ אֹתָהּ.

Jacob worked seven years for Rachel and they seemed to
him a few days because of his love for her.

Genesis 29:20

There is a famous story about a student who accompanies
his rabbi to a restaurant for dinner. After they are seated
and have looked over the menu, the rabbi asks, "What
would you like to eat?" Still scanning the options, the
student responds, "I love fish, so…" The rabbi interrupts
by gently lowering the student's menu, makes eye contact,
and corrects them: "If you really love fish, you would let it
live out its life peacefully in the water. Instead, you are
willing to pay someone to catch it, kill it, dice it, deep fry
the pieces, and then you will eat it. You don't love fish.
You love the way eating fish makes you feel."

Love can be selfish or selfless. We can love another, God
forbid, for what the person can provide to us - or we can

love by trying to offer as much as possible. In Hebrew, the word for "love" is אהבה. It comes from the root הב, which means "to give." In the purest kind of love, we seek to better ourselves as a way of making the best possible offering to those we love.

In our *parsha*, the Torah testifies that Jacob's love was **for** Rachel. Perhaps that is why the seven long years of labor felt like days for him.[1] Moments waiting for a beloved can feel like an eternity, but Jacob was already achieving a sense of closeness in the moment by investing the time to work and refine himself. It is not coincidental that he, like many of our early leaders, was first a shepherd of animals before leading people.[2] Putting the needs of others first isn't easy, and it took effort for these leaders to habituate themselves to accommodating the needs of their flock.

The Jerusalem Talmud[3] teaches that we can best learn how to love another by learning to love ourselves and then expanding from there. The rabbis explain the connection between the first half of the verse "You shall not seek revenge" with the second half of the verse, "You shall love your neighbor as yourself"[4] through a parable of a person who accidentally cut their finger while preparing food. Would the wounded hand take the knife and avenge itself by stabbing the hand that cut it? When we understand ourselves as being part of a greater whole, this not only

---

[1] See Mishnas Reb Aharon for a fuller explanation.
[2] See the Alter of Slabodka.
[3] Jerusalem Talmud Nedarim 30b.
[4] Leviticus 19:18.

30

discourages revenge, but it can inspire deep love. We are all commanded to love another the way that we love ourselves, but if we are not aware of the care we need to offer ourselves, we can end up hurting others.

Before we can expand our concern to include others, we need to understand our own needs. The way that we feel about ourselves can teach us how to properly feel for others. We must love ourselves in order to fully love someone else. Jacob is successful in archiving this level of love, even in his complicated relationship with his brother, through grace.[5]

This is especially true in our most intimate relationships. Maimonides teaches that one must honor one's partner even more than one honors oneself, and they should love their partner as much as they love themselves.[6] The source for this is the Babylonian Talmud,[7] but it is noteworthy that the order there is reversed: One must love their partner the way one loves oneself and should honor their partner even more.[8] The rabbis explain that Maimonides changes the order because he is offering practical advice on how to cultivate love for another. The first step is understanding and honoring what is important to the other, and then making it important to you.

---

[5] Pri Tzadik Shemos 10:1 describing their dynamic as וזהו מציאת חן מרצון הרצוניות מעתיקא.

[6] וְכֵן צִוּוּ חֲכָמִים שֶׁיִּהְיֶה אָדָם מְכַבֵּד אֶת אִשְׁתּוֹ יוֹתֵר מִגּוּפוֹ וְאוֹהֲבָהּ כְּגוּפוֹ.

[7] Bavli Yevamot 62b.

[8] ת"ר האוהב את אשתו כגופו והמכבדה יותר מגופו.

Tradition also acknowledges that desire is natural, powerful, and needs to be harnessed and channeled. The mystics understand the 613 commandments in the Torah as corresponding to 613 parts of our being.[9] The commandment of loving another as we love ourselves is connected to the part of us that experiences desire. Intimate relationships offer the unique opportunity to focus on the needs of another, with as much sensitivity as if those needs were one's own. It is for this reason that the Talmud mandates that one see the other before marrying, to make sure there is an attraction; the Torah's imperative to love another as oneself is given as the prooftext.[10]

Jacob's love for Rachel is passionate and generous. His work, both internal and external, models how we can find personal nourishment by focusing on the needs of another. God wants us to feel loved, and to know that we will never get there by exploiting others. Instead, we attain love through offering it in healthy ways.

---

[9] See Bavli Makkot 23b and Zohar 1:170b.
[10] There are more rational reasons to be attractive to one's partner, as Maimonides writes: otherwise the partnership could end in graceless hate, or divorce. וְלֹא יְקַדֵּשׁ אִשָּׁה עַד שֶׁיִּרְאֶנָּה וְתִהְיֶה כְּשֵׁרָה בְּעֵינָיו שֶׁמָּא לֹא תִּמְצָא חֵן בְּעֵינָיו וְנִמְצָא מְגָרְשָׁהּ אוֹ שׁוֹכֵב עִמָּהּ וְהוּא שׂוֹנְאָהּ.

Vayishlach - Graceful Being

וַיָּבֹא יַעֲקֹב שָׁלֵם עִיר שְׁכֶם, אֲשֶׁר בְּאֶרֶץ כְּנַעַן, בְּבֹאוֹ, מִפַּדַּן
אֲרָם; וַיִּחַן, אֶת-פְּנֵי הָעִיר.

And Jacob came in peace to the city of Shechem, which is
in the land of Canaan, when he came from Paddan-aram;
and encamped before the city.

Genesis 33:18

"Don't just do something, stand there." The White Rabbit
in *Alice in Wonderland* understands that human beings have
a very hard time just being. Often it is easier to pursue the
future, and be distracted from the moment, than to be
fully in the present. But it is really important for us to "just
be" sometimes. When we are only thinking about what is
next, our ability to actually improve ourselves is
diminished.

Every week, *shabbos* invites us to pivot from a weekday
posture of creative production to one of graceful existence.
(From "doing something" to "just being.") The *medresh*
teaches that Jacob came to the city of Shechem on *erev*

shabbos, and prepared for the day of rest. The Sefas Emes understands the word "ויחן", in the context of this verse, not just as "he encamped," but also that Jacob restored grace, חן, to the land.

Sefer Yetzirah teaches that God connects the letter ת with both חן/grace and *shabbos*. As a result, *shabbos* is inherently filled with grace. *Shabbos* supports our acquisition of grace by giving us the opportunity to reflect on what we have and to be satisfied with it. Just as God rested on *shabbos* from creation and appreciated what had been made, so too *shabbos* provides us with a weekly reminder to cease pursuing the physical and instead to elevate it to a level of spirituality.

The brothers Jacob and Esav offer two different ways of relating to "what we have" and "enoughness." When Jacob is on his way to meet Esav, he attempts to make amends with his brother by sending him many gifts. Esav rejects the offering, saying, "I have plenty," which Rashi understands as an arrogant boast of accomplishment. By contrast, Jacob says of himself, "I have all (כל)," which Rashi interprets to mean that he has enough.

Jacob tells Esav, "כִּי-חַנַּנִי אֱלֹקים וְכִי יֶשׁ-לִי-כֹל" / "God has been gracious to me and therefore I have all that I need."[1] He means, "I have found the Godly type of grace, not a superficial one." Jacob wants to give Esav not only

---

[1] Genesis 33:11.

physical gifts, but also the holy gift of an elevated worldview; knowing that what one has is enough.

Esav comes with 400 men, a representation of the force of "רע עין," a negative outlook on the world. Jacob lives for 147 years, which corresponds to the numerical value of "עין טוב," a positive outlook on the world. The numerical value of "יש לי כל," I have enough, is 400, the same as the letter "ת" which as we explained, is connected to *shabbos* and to חן/grace. Jacob was modeling for his brother a practice of being satisfied with what one has, and not being distracted by the superficial pleasure of being seen as successful through excess. This reflects a real internal חן/grace.[2]

"וַיָּבֹא יַעֲקֹב שָׁלֵם," Jacob came *shalem*, in peace. שָׁלֵם/s*halem* can also mean complete or full. Jacob came on erev *shabbos*, a time of completion. We conclude physical work before *shabbos* so that we can be free to invest in the spiritual "work" of *shabbos*.[3] *Shabbos*'s name is *shalom*.[4] Part of achieving graceful living is appreciating what we have, existing in Jacob's state of יש לי כל. For the moment we know that we have all we need.

---

[2] חיצון = חן יופי.
[3] עיין אמרי אמת תר"צ, בשבת אדם משלים עצמו.
[4] See Zohar Chadash, Bereshit 718.

Vayeishev - Graceful Education

וַיִּרְאוּ אֶחָיו, כִּי-אֹתוֹ אָהַב אֲבִיהֶם מִכָּל-אֶחָיו–וַיִּשְׂנְאוּ, אֹתוֹ; וְלֹא
יָכְלוּ, דַּבְּרוֹ לְשָׁלֹם

His brothers saw that it was he whom their father loved
most of all his brothers so they hated him and were not
able to speak to him peacefully.

Genesis 37:4

This coming week we begin to celebrate the eight day
festival of Chanukah. The Beis Yosef[1] famously asks: Why
are there eight days? If there was only enough oil for the
first day, wasn't the miracle in fact for just 7 days? Why
then isn't the festival just seven days long?

One of my favorite answers is supplied by the *baalei mussar*.
They teach that indeed everything in the world is
miraculous. We are just so accustomed to everyday
wonders that we call them "natural". If God willed for

---

[1] R' Yosef Caro (1488 - 1575) Toledo then Israel.

water to burn and oil to extinguish, then our "normal" would be perceived as the supernatural. Chanukah is a time to question what is real, and what we've simply accepted as truth because we are used to it. On Chanukah we acknowledge and appreciate the hidden light in the seemingly mundane.

This week's *parsha* is also one of hidden light. People who are discounted, rejected, and dismissed turn out to be the mainstays of redemption. Joseph, the younger brother, is thrown into a pit, nearly killed, and sold as a slave; but he then becomes the viceroy of Egypt and is able to save everyone from famine. According to the *medrash*, after Shechem violates Dina, she becomes pregnant and gives birth to Asnos. Dina's brothers want to abandon the baby, but Jacob intervenes and arranges for her to be adopted by an Egyptian family. This baby girl, according to the *medrash*, grows up and marries Joseph. Together they parent Menashe and Efraim, the first brothers to ever get along with each other, in the Bible. This light, hidden below the surface, is able to shine and to disturb the system of artificially evaluating human worth; the system that discounted both Joseph and Dina.

So too with Tamar. Yehuda wanted to execute her because he assumed that she had become pregnant through harlotry, when he himself was in fact the father. When Tamar reveals the truth to Yehuda, he declares that she is more righteous than he. Tradition teaches that the Messiah of the Davidic line is descended from Tamar, while the Messiah of Joseph's line comes from Asnos. (Yes, tradition speaks of more than one redeemer.) What's important here is that each of these figures is descended from someone who was considered unworthy of living, but survived and became a necessary agent of salvation … just like Joseph.

In the times of the Chanukah story, when men were passive in the face of evil decrees and bride trafficking, it was Yehudis who had faith in the power of change. She resisted, rebelled, and revolted. Chanukah is the only Jewish holiday that falls during two different months, demonstrating its own ability to incorporate shifts in the changing of time.

The name Chanukah comes from the language of *chinuch*, education. Now, as during the Chanukah story, we must actively pursue a constant re-education about what is right and appropriate. One of the indicators that we are being successful is whether or not we are producing *chein*, gracefulness,[2] also at the root of both words.

The Greeks wanted us to forget the Torah and its eternal truth: that real power doesn't rest in physical strength or gatherings of men, but in the One who "delivered the strong into the hands of the weak, the many into the hands of the few."[3] The candles that we light each night remind us of our partnership with the Divine and the source of holiness that is our most precious resource.

We live in very dark times, but contained within is the hidden light. The *medrash* teaches that while everyone was busying themselves in these painful narratives, God was

---

[2] חנוכה גימטריא חן א-ל Chanukah has the same numerical value of "Godly grace".
[3] Liturgical insert for Chanukah.

involved in creating the light of redemption. When we challenge structures that support oppressors, we are shining the light of truth that is the most disruptive to the lies of evil. The rebellions of today's resistance are no less miraculous or courageous, perhaps they just feel more natural.

Mikeitz - Graceful Rising

וַיֹּאמֶר–הִנֵּה שָׁמַעְתִּי, כִּי יֶשׁ-שֶׁבֶר בְּמִצְרָיִם; רְדוּ-שָׁמָּה וְשִׁבְרוּ-
לָנוּ מִשָּׁם, וְנִחְיֶה וְלֹא נָמוּת

And [Jacob] said. "Behold, I have heard that there are
provisions in Egypt; go down there and purchase for us
from there, so that we may live and not die.

Genesis 42:2

This week's *parsha* finds Jacob in a difficult time. He is in
deep mourning for his son Joseph, a serious famine has
descended upon the region, and Jacob and his remaining
sons are in danger of starvation. Amid these struggles,
Jacob bids his sons to take a treacherous journey to Egypt
following the prospect of food. The *medrash* is bothered by
Jacob's use of the word "שבר" for food. Why not use אכל,
which would be a more common term?[1] The *medrash*
answers that Jacob wanted to convey an aspect of hope.
The root שבר appears in psalms with a connotation of

---

[1] Berishis Rabbah 91:6.

— אַשְׁרֵי שֶׁאֵל יַעֲקֹב בְּעֶזְרוֹ שִׂבְרוֹ עַל־יְהוָה אֱלֹהָיו :optimism
Happy is the one who has the God of Jacob for help,
whose hope is in the Lord their God.[2]

Jacob tells his sons, "רדו שמה"—descend there. The word
"רדו" has the numerical value of 210, which is an allusion
to the 210 years of enslavement in Egypt.[3] This trip down
to Egypt is emblematic of future struggles. Faith in our
ability to create positive change nourishes the movement
of the moment to arrive at the destination on the other
side of the descent. "There"—שמה—has the same letters
as משה, Moses, teaching us that after the 210 years there
will be liberation, the giving of the Torah, and freedom.[4]

The word שבר can also mean brokenness. It's easy to
experience brokenness as hopelessness, but our rabbis
embrace it as a process of humility and empowerment.
When things are difficult, we are easily tempted to give up.
It takes a unique strength, entwined with a particular grace
to descend into the darkness and fight for light and life.
The miracle of Chanukah is, that in the aftermath of
horrific trauma, we didn't surrender or stop searching for
light.[5] We went down into the shattered fragments, and
came out elevated on a supernal plane.

---

[2] Psalms 146:5.
[3] Rashi quoting Midrash Rabbah.
[4] עיין צמח צדיק.
[5] One reason why Chanukah is eight days is that we are
celebrating the miracle of the searching itself.

We are told that things do get better, but we are rarely aware of where we are in the arc of it all. Being created in the Divine Image means that we, like God, have the ability to create new realities. The power of our impact is so great that we must constantly be alert and cautious. We are taught: "Do not believe in yourself [that you will always get it right] until the day of your death; for Rabbi Yochonon was the High Priest in the Temple for 80 years, but at the end of his life he denied Divine authority."[6] Even someone who seems to be doing everything right might make mistakes, and even someone who seems to be doing everything wrong can always improve.

The Chanukah liturgy recalls the brave actions of Matisyahu ben Yochonon, the High Priest, who led the resistance against the Greeks.[7] There is a tradition that Matisyahu is the son of the High Priest who rebelled. His actions that we celebrate on Chanukah are the corrective act that restores our faith in the Divine and repairs his father's mistake. As a result of his efforts to fix what was broken we now have another mitzvah in the Oral Law, and he is seen as an embodiment of (*ben*) his father's true identity of grace.[8] (The word chein, grace, is hidden within the name Yochanan/יוחנן.[9])

---

[6] Bavli Brachos 29a.

[7] עיין בני יששכר מ"ד כה.

[8] שם כד.

[9] It is noteworthy that the three letters that remain, without חן/grace, spell Yavan/יו, the Hebrew word for Greece, and demonstrate a literal descent, as Hebrew is read from right to left.

Matisyahu was committed to a more perfect existence, reminiscent of the story of Rabbi Elezer ben Dordiah.[10] At the end of his life, Rabbi Eliezer ben Dordiah recognized all of the desecration and defilement that he had caused, and his transformation triggered a revolt of holiness and sanctification that the physical limitations of the earthly world could no longer contain, manifesting the miraculous.[11] His internal change came about through grace. So too, later in this week's *parsha*, when Joseph raises his eyes to his brother Benjamin, and asks God to bless him with grace.[12] The mystical tradition sees this as a blessing for Chanukah. Grace allows us to rededicate ourselves to hopefulness and spiritual pursuits.[13]

---

[10] Tractate Avoda Zarah 17a: Rabbi Elezer ben Dordiah spent his life exploiting women for pleasure and after traveling the world pursuing physical indulgence he repents from such a depth that his soul leaves his body and is ushered into heaven with a Divine Voice calling him Rabbi.

[11] The Ari z"l taught (פרע״ח) that he was a reincarnation of Yochanan Kohen Gadol.

[12] 43:29.

[13] Meor Yenayim.

Vayigash - Graceful Responsibility

וְלֹא־יָכֹל יוֹסֵף לְהִתְאַפֵּק, לְכֹל הַנִּצָּבִים עָלָיו, וַיִּקְרָא, הוֹצִיאוּ כָל-
אִישׁ מֵעָלָי; וְלֹא-עָמַד אִישׁ אִתּוֹ, בְּהִתְוַדַּע יוֹסֵף אֶל-אֶחָיו

Joseph could no longer control himself before all his attendants, and he cried out, "Have everyone withdraw from me!" So there was no one else about when Joseph made himself known to his brothers.

Genesis 45:1

One of the most dramatic moments in the Genesis narrative is when Joseph reveals himself to his brothers declaring: "I am Joseph. Is my father still alive?" The *medrash* explains that it was Judah who brought Joseph to a point where he could hold back no longer and therefore divulged his true identity. Rabbi Chiya bar Abba[1] posits that Judah's speech, although directed at Joseph, is actually

---

[1] Third century Israel.

constructed to appease Joseph, Benjamin, and the other brothers.

We understand why Judah needs to apologize to Joseph and Benjamin. It was Judah's plan to sell Joseph as a slave, upending Joseph's life and robbing Benjamin of his only brother from the same mother. But it is interesting that Rabbi Chiya thinks that Judah is appeasing his other brothers as well. The other brothers had wanted to kill Joseph, while Judah suggested they could make some money by selling Joseph as a slave. Judah could argue that his other brothers are equally complicit in what was done to Joseph, but instead he chooses to take full responsibility for the situation.

In a relationship, it is an act of grace to take responsibility for our actions and inactions without trying to share the blame. Our choices are meaningful because they represent our will, and as a result they are ours to own. We should make it a daily practice to take stock of our deeds, but Yom Kippur is especially designated as a particular Day of Reckoning in the Jewish calendar. The High Priest in the Yom Kippur temple service takes full responsibility for the deeds of Israel. He is compared on this day to a graceful groom, reflecting the magnanimous nature of his behavior and the joy of the experience.

The *medrash* says that the meal which precipitated Joseph's revelation happened on *shabbos*. *Shabbos* is a time when we are able to access and orient ourselves to the truth of being God's creations. The Hebrew word for face, פנים, is the same as the word for "inside" because the face gives expression to what is going on internally within a person.

Our rabbis teach that the light that emanates from a person's face is different on *shabbos* than during the week, and has its source in the holiness of the Garden of Eden. Even Adam, after the sin, didn't lose that light until Saturday night. *Shabbos* invites us to remember and take action. To return to the ideal and work to fix the things we have broken.

The brothers are rendered speechless by Joseph's revelation. The *medrash* uses this as a model for us and our own day of reckoning: "Woe to us on the day of judgment, woe to us on the day of rebuke."[2] If the brothers were not able to answer Joseph, how are we going to be able to answer God?

Joseph did not rebuke his brothers; he simply revealed the truth of the situation. *Chein*/grace can be understood as an acronym for *chochma nistera*/hidden wisdom. The brothers had originally thought that Joseph was extraneous and expendable. The "judgment" came with Joseph simply letting them know that they had gotten it wrong.

On the Day of Judgement we will all be confronted by the truth of our potential. This prospect is terrifying. When people become aware of their failings, they can feel embarrassed and even give up hope of correcting bad behavior. *Chein* is the ability to see the greatness of the hidden and bring it out. The groom, on the verge of marriage, epitomizes embracing one's potential and turning it into reality. It is that commitment to the ideal

---

[2] Bereishis Rabbah 93:10.

that empowers the groom to take responsibility for the inevitable bumps along the way. Acknowledging our mistakes allows us to make amends for the past and better positions us for a more perfect future.

Vayechi - Charismatic Grace

בֵּן פֹּרָת יוֹסֵף, בֵּן פֹּרָת עֲלֵי-עָיִן; בָּנוֹת, צָעֲדָה עֲלֵי-שׁוּר.

A charming son is Joseph, a charming son to the eye; each of the daughters climbed heights to gaze.

Genesis 49:22

Although Joseph[1] was aware of his exceptional desirability, he never relied on his good looks, the privilege of being Jacob and Rachel's oldest son, or on the financial success or political power that he accrued in Egypt. We read in Psalms that "praise worthy is the person who has made Hashem their trust".[2] According to the *medrash*, this to Joseph.[3] He is the paradigm of a person who trusts in God. When the baker and the cup-bearer are disturbed by their dreams, Joseph tells them, "God has all dream

---

[1] Rabbanu B'Chaya (28:15) writes that שוהם - onyx is מסוגל for grace and for that reason Joseph's name is written on this stone for the breast plate.
[2] Psalms 40:5.
[3] Berishis Rabbah 9:3.

interpretations."[4] When Joseph is later summoned to explain Pharaoh's dreams, he declares, "It is not me. God will answer the peace of Pharaoh."[5]

Yet, the same *medrash* faults Joseph for asking the cup-bearer twice[6] to help him get out of prison. Because Joseph relied on a person, by asking for their intervention, instead of just having faith in God, he was forced to spend an additional two years in prison; one for each of the requests. However, it is implied that, had he only asked once, he wouldn't have been punished at all. So why isn't Joseph simply sentenced to one year, for the single unnecessary ask?

This *medrash* highlights one of the paradoxes of living a life of faith. Faith can be a propelling force that drives a person to seek and effect change, or it can comfort a person with the belief that everything will be ok so they don't need to act. How can we balance our belief that God will cause everything to turn out as it should, with the imperative to try our hardest to accomplish what we can? Wasn't it proper for Joseph to try to get himself released from jail? Shouldn't we always try to improve our situation without sitting back and waiting for God to make it better?

Faith, or *bitachon* in Hebrew, enabled Joseph to tell his brothers time and again[7] that it was God's plan that he go down to Egypt. Rashi translates "a charming son" as "a

---

[4] Genesis 40:8.
[5] Genesis 41:16.
[6] Genesis 40:14.
[7] Genesis 45:8, Genesis 50:20.

son of grace/ *chein*." *Bitachon*/בטחון, is an anagram of טוב
חן—good grace. Jealousy only exists in the absence of faith
in God's wisdom and oversight. If we really believe that
God has given each of us what we need to fulfill our
unique purpose in this world, how could we possibly want
what another has?

Our rabbis point out that the Hebrew word for "worry" is
dayga, דאגה, which has four of the first five letters of the
Hebrew alphabet, and is just missing the *bet*/ב, for *bitachon*.
It is that *bet*/ב that we find as the first letter of Genesis.
The stories in Genesis, known as *aggadah*/אגדה (those
same four letters again), help inspire our faith, reduce our
anxiety, and build the foundation for our relationship with
God and each other.

The Gra says that the large "ב" in the first word of the
Torah, "בראשית/In the beginning," represents "בטחון,"
faith. He further teaches that the first word can be parsed
as "בראש-ית," at the head of "ית," an allusion to the three
letters in the Hebrew alphabet that head/precede "ית":
namely ב,ט,ח.[8] Together, these three letters form the root
of "faith"—in Hebrew, בטחון—which can be understood
as God's promise of our committed relationship.[9] Joseph
was in an exceedingly intimate dynamic with God and he
lived with a deep awareness of God. But the moment he
diverted his focus to another, he lapsed in that
consciousness of God - to the extent that it was clear to

---

[8] בית, טית, חית.
[9] תי = 410 = קדוש.

God that even the first time he asked the cupbearer for help, he had the wrong motivation, and was therefore held responsible for both requests.

Motivation matters. Our relationship with God matters. We never lose by doing the right thing. If we believe that God is the Source of everything, how could we possibly advance our position by going against the will of the Creator, hurting another person, or misusing our resources for selfish gains? Each one of us has a connection to God, the Torah, and each other. We must see ourselves as partners and coworkers in the elevation of it all - and, like Joseph, allow our charming and grace-filled faith to sustain us in the work of healing this broken world together.

Sefer Shemot

Shemos - Graceful Allyship

וַיְהִי בַּיָּמִים הָהֵם, וַיִּגְדַּל מֹשֶׁה וַיֵּצֵא אֶל-אֶחָיו, וַיַּרְא, בְּסִבְלֹתָם; וַיַּרְא אִישׁ מִצְרִי, מַכֶּה אִישׁ-עִבְרִי מֵאֶחָיו.

It happened in those days that Moshe grew up and went out to his brethren and saw their burdens; and he saw an Egyptian man striking a Hebrew man, of his brethren.

Exodus 2:11

Despite the brutal enslavement of his people, Moshe grew up safely cocooned in Pharaoh's household. As the adopted son of Pharaoh's daughter, Moshe was protected from the torment and endless labors of Israel. Yet, as he grew older, Moshe chose to turn away from his own comfort to see his siblings' suffering.

Moshe's evolution is heart-centered. Rashi explains that he "placed his eyes and heart to be distressed over them."[1] In

---

[1] נָתַן עֵינָיו וְלִבּוֹ לִהְיוֹת מֵצַר עֲלֵיהֶם.

not averting, but aligning his eyes and heart, Moshe united against their oppression; his allyship was the natural consequence of feeling the connectivity of humanity.

We find this reflected in the prayer that we offer during the Torah service: אַחֵינוּ כָּל בֵּית יִשְׂרָאֵל הַנְּתוּנִים בַּצָּרָה/As for our brethren, the entire House of Israel who remain in distress and captivity… Although the entire people are not literally "all in distress,"[2] the pain of the individual is the pain of the whole, and we must all feel it personally.

This act of allyship was not without a cost; it came at the expense of Moshe's own privilege. Medrash Tanchuma relates that Pharaoh had put Moshe in charge of the royal household. Yet, when Moshe aligns himself with the suffering of others and defends them from the cruel taskmaster, Pharaoh turns on him and Moshe is forced to flee. In just three verses Moshe goes from running Pharaoh's affairs to being on the run himself, fearing for his own life.[3]

The story reads as if Moshe lost the option of working from within and being an agent of change, but in truth it was this act that allowed him to be worthy of true impact. The *medrash* sees Moshe's focus on the enslaved Hebrew both as the singular act that merited his unique closeness to God, and also as part of a daily spiritual practice of micro-affections.

---

[2] Zahav Misveh.
[3] Rashi 2:11.

He was subversive, and his subversiveness was an act of resistance.

The *medrash*[4] comments on our verse: "'And he looked on their burdens.' What is, 'And he looked?' For he would look upon their burdens and cry and say, 'Woe is me unto you, who will provide my death instead of yours…' Rabbi Eliezer the son of Rabbi Yose the Galilean said: [If] he saw a large burden on a small person and a small burden on a large person, or a man's burden on a woman and a woman's burden on a man, or an elderly man's burden on a young man and a young man's burden on an elderly man, he would leave aside his rank and go and right their burdens, and act as though he were assisting Pharaoh."

Moshe's intervention is seen by the rabbis as the act that merited God's reciprocity of divine intervention. "The Holy One Blessed is God said: You left aside your business and went to see the sorrow of Israel, and acted toward them as brothers act. I will leave aside the upper and the lower [i.e. ignore the distinction between Heaven and Earth] and talk to you." Such is it written, "And when the LORD saw that [Moses] turned aside to see."[5] God saw Moses, who left aside his business to see their burdens. Therefore, "God called unto him out of the midst of the bush."[6]

---

[4] Shemot Rabbah 1:27.
[5] Exodus 3:4.
[6] Shemot Rabbah 1:27.

Moshe eventually became the spokesperson for God because of his heart-forward posture. King Solomon alludes to in the verse: אֹהֵב טהור לֵב חֵן שְׂפָתָיו, רֵעֵהוּ מֶלֶךְ "A pure-hearted friend, his speech is gracious; he has the King for his companion."[7] The King in this verse is a reference to God,[8] and the "friend" refers to Moshe, whose grace-filled speech enables him to be God's companion.[9] The sincerity of Moses's heart made his speech graceful. His heart and mouth were aligned with each other. Flattery, חנף, by contrast, is the additional disingenuous speech, פה, with superficial grace/חן.[10]

The voice of an ally must originate in the heart as an internal response to whatever agonizing humanitarian failure one is witnessing. It also empowers us to speak truth to power. The heart is a muscle that requires work and watchfulness to develop. We are taught[11] that the entire purpose of every mitzvah is to fix and restore the heart.[12] Indeed, immediately after Moshe flees Pharaoh we are told about his activism at the well, which came from the same source of advocacy.[13]

This week, we start reading the book of Exodus and the atrocities of enslavement, torment and infanticide. The Bal

---

[7] Proverbs 22:11.

[8] Gra.

[9] Bamidbar Rabbah 15.

[10] ר.מ.ד. ואלי.

[11] Kad HaKemach, Shavuot 1:2.

[12] ודבר ידוע כי כל מצות שבתורה אינן אלא לתקן הלב כי הלב הוא העיקר.

[13] Exodus 2:15-16.

Haturim observes that the first word, "שמות", is an acronym for שְׁנַיִם מִקְרָא וְאֶחָד תַּרְגּוּם, the rabbinic directive to read the weekly Torah portion twice in Hebrew and once in translation.[14] The commentaries are curious about the placement of this teaching: why here?

There is often an urge to try and avoid, and even deny, uncomfortable or difficult realities. Perhaps the timing of this reminder is especially critical here to instruct us that when we are made aware of injustices—our own or others—we should not turn away but instead look closer, and then look again, to understand why it happened, and to make sure it stops and never happens again.

Parashat Shemos also begins a period of time known as "*shovavim*," an acronym of the upcoming Torah portions, meaning to return. Central to this story of development and maturity is a shift from self-focus to caring for others. These weeks collectively narrate the birth and growth of the Jewish nation and the evolution of Moshe as the Israelites' leader. In recounting both Moshe's and the Jewish people's progress, this story provides us with the scaffolding to support our own work as individuals, encumbered by the needs of the community.[15] Redemption comes when we love others as ourselves, not as others.

---

[14] ש.מ.ו.ת. שְׁנַיִם מִקְרָא וְאֶחָד תַּרְגּוּם.
[15] "Shovavim" has the numerical value of "oppression" and worry. שובבים = מיצר ודואג.

Va'eira - Graceful Consolation

וַיְדַבֵּר מֹשֶׁה כֵּן, אֶל-בְּנֵי יִשְׂרָאֵל; וְלֹא שָׁמְעוּ, אֶל-מֹשֶׁה, מִקֹּצֶר
רוּחַ, וּמֵעֲבֹדָה קָשָׁה.

But when Moses told this to the Israelites, they did not
listen to Moses, because of shortness of breath and hard
work.

Exodus 6:9

Although this *parsha* brings with it the good news of
liberation, the Israelites were not positioned to hear it.
They couldn't be comforted, because they could not yet
imagine a reality different from the one they were currently
experiencing. The struggle for freedom and equality must
include breaking the limitations in our minds around what
is possible. This process of introspection is an essential
stage in alleviating the pain of the moment and moving
towards a better future.

Rashi explains that the Israelites were not consoled by
Moshe's promises of redemption. In Hebrew, the word for
consolation, נחם, is the same as "reconsider." In the time

of Noah, before the flood, God reconsidered having made people and was pained.[1] Rashi explains that God was consoled in part by remembering that at least humanity's destruction was limited to this world. Consolation involves consideration of different possibilities, and it is precisely this flexibility of thought that eluded Israel and left them comfortless.

We are told, in the Talmud,[2] that for several years the Houses of Hillel and Shammai argued whether it was better for humanity to have been created or not. Finally, they concluded that "Better to not have been created than to have been created, but now that we have been created we should examine our deeds." The rabbis understand this teaching both as a reminder that the world that God created - in the garden before the sin - was perfect and well worth creating, and that our current world - the consequence of our mistakes - can be restored to perfection by working on ourselves and on society.

Sometimes it is hard to hear that things will ever be different or could even get better. In general, the descriptive words we use are rarely as expansive as experiences themselves, especially regarding events that haven't happened yet. Perhaps this is why God uses four different expressions of redemption: והוצאתי, והצלתי וגאלתי, ולקחתי.[3]

---

[1] Genesis 6:6.
[2] Bavli Eruvin 13b.
[3] To take out, rescue, redeem, and take you.

Aspiring for a better future helps us get there. Ruth was able to see and appreciate the good, despite the severe difficulties of her life as a penniless widow. She says to Boaz, "May I continue to find favor, חֵן, in your eyes because you have comforted me and you spoke to my heart."[4] Ruth can hear Boaz's words of comfort and be affected by them. She knows that a better future is possible. Indeed, the *medrash* on this verse comments that she isn't to be seen as a maidservant, הָאֲמָהוֹת, but as a matriarch, הָאִמָּהוֹת. The only difference between these two labels is the point of perspective.

In this week's Torah portion, we are told about the birth of Pinchas, who is traditionally associated with Elijah the prophet, the bearer of the good news of the future. In the daily grace after meals, we pray: הָרַחֲמָן הוּא יִשְׁלַח לָנוּ אֶת־ אֵלִיָּהוּ הַנָּבִיא זָכוּר לַטּוֹב, וִיבַשֶּׂר־לָנוּ בְּשׂוֹרוֹת טוֹבוֹת יְשׁוּעוֹת וְנֶחָמוֹת.

"The Merciful One will send us Elijah the prophet, who is remembered for good, who will announce to us good tidings, deliverances, and consolations."

We acknowledge and welcome Elijah's presence at the Passover seder and even have a 5th cup of wine for him in recognition of the redemption that we still need to work towards. By doing so, we open ourselves up to comfort and to the possibility of redemption.

---

[4] Ruth 2:14.

Our ancestors were enslaved for 210 years and failed to envision a different existence. We have now been in exile for nearly 2000 years, and we are still more connected to mourning our loss than we are to rebuilding what was lost. The reason for the Temple's destruction - blatant hatred - seems to only intensify by the day. We must be able to look at this sad reality, at least in part, with an optimistic lens - so we can see that contained in this separation is a path towards reunification and true healing.

Bo - Graceful Control

וְהָיָה לְךָ לְאוֹת עַל-יָדְךָ, וּלְזִכָּרוֹן בֵּין עֵינֶיךָ, לְמַעַן תִּהְיֶה תּוֹרַת
ה', בְּפִיךָ: כִּי בְּיָד חֲזָקָה, הוֹצִאֲךָ ה' מִמִּצְרָיִם.

And it will be for you a sign on your hand and for
remembrance between your eyes so that God's Torah may
be in your mouth; for with a strong hand God removed
you from Egypt.

Exodus 13:9

Speech is most powerful when it is simultaneously
controlled and free. We need the liberty to express
ourselves, but if we do not exert care and restraint in what
we say, our words cannot be optimally effective.
Tefillin/טוטפות, an expression of speech,[1] is the first daily
mitzvah commanded in the Torah and a model of both
freedom and constraint. We bind ourselves to God's

---

[1] Rashi, Exodus 13:16.

words with leather straps, and in doing so we exercise free choice to demonstrate a powerful religious commitment.

The purpose of tefillin is לְמַעַן תִּהְיֶה תוֹרַת ה' בְּפִיךָ, so that our mouths will be filled with Torah. Tefillin is understood as a covenant of our mouths.[2] Even though tefillin contain the words of the Written Torah, they are a symbol of the Oral Torah as well.

Tradition teaches that this commandment was delivered on the eve of Passover, right before the Exodus from Egypt, as partial preparation for the redemption of speech. The Hebrew word for Egypt, מצרים, like the text of the Talmud, starts and ends with the letter מ/mem. The Talmud teaches[3] that the "מ"[4] is sometimes open and sometimes closed (a regular mem has an opening; a final mem is a closed shape) to demonstrate that while some things should be said, others should remain unsaid, behind closed mouths. The first letter in the text of the Mishnah, and in the word Mitzrayim, is open while the last letter in both is closed. The letters that remain in Mitzrayim form the word "desire"/יצר/*yetzer*.

Another name for the *yetzer*[5] is *michshol*/מכשיל/to stumble.[6] When one wraps the straps of tefillin around the

---

[2] עיין שפת אמת פ' נח תרנ"ד.

[3] Bavli Shabbos 104a.

[4] Spelled מם with both letters, the first "open" and last "closed".

[5] עיין בן יהוידע ברכות ה: רע עין = 400 on the story of 400 barrels of wine that turned to vinegar.

[6] Michsol also has a numerical value of 400, the same as ת in חתן, leaving חן remaining.

ring finger and recites, "I will betroth you to me
forever…with faithfulness," it should be with the joy of a
groom under the chuppah.[7] Vilna Gaon says the two *shin*s,
"ש," on the tefillin form the word *sus*, the root of
ששון/celebration. In relationships, we commit to renewing
our identity as a *chason*/groom and should remind
ourselves of the need for self control to prevent falling
short.

The rabbis fear that emotions, even joyous ones, can
become too expansive and cause us to stumble. Rabbah
noticed that Abaye was exceedingly happy and said to him:
"rejoice with trepidation!"[8] Abaye responded by saying, "I
am wearing tefillin."[9] The Gemara then continues with the
story of Mar, who made a wedding feast for his son and
thought the rabbis were having too good of a time. He
bought an expensive glass that was worth 400 *zuz*[10] and
broke it in front of them, to contain their joy. This,
according to Tosafot, is why we have the universal custom
of breaking a glass at weddings.[11]

There are several differences between the tefillin of the
arm and the head. The one worn on the head, like the
intellect, is compartmentalized. There are four separate

---

[7] Malbim Hosea 2:21 כמ"ש ומשוש חתן על כלה ישיש עליך
אלהיך, ויהיו אירוסין חדשים.
[8] Psalms 2:11.
[9] Brachos 30b.
[10] Also an allusion to Esev who came after Jacob with 400 men.
[11] The Tzlach explains that we are similar to glass in that we are
also made from the earth and that if we fall and break (through
sin) we can also be reformed, like glass, through repentance.

texts, each in their own space, like the four senses of sight, hearing, taste, and smell; each having their own domain. By contrast, the one on the arm corresponds to the heart and like our emotions, is total. The one on our head is revealed, and the one on the arm concealed, to remind us of the need to process our feelings into words that are appropriate for another to hear.

The ways in which we interact with others says a lot about who we are. Our ability to control ourselves and act properly testifies about our character, especially in emotionally charged situations.[12] Maturity has been defined as the intellect's ability to control the emotions and support a healthy balance of the two.[13]

With the Exodus from Egypt came the birth of a people and the need to relearn how to speak properly. The word Passover in Hebrew is פסח: "Peh Sach," a mouth that speaks. All of the *mitzvos* of the seder—telling the story, eating matzah, drinking wine - involve the mouth. Pharaoh is understood as פה רע/"Peh Rah"/the evil mouth. The more we fill ourselves with Torah, the more empowered we are. For there is no freedom when we are not in control, especially control over the words that come out of our mouth.

---

[12] In the verse of Shema, the first and last letters are large and form the word עד, meaning testimony. The Gra observes that the remaining letters in those two words form אשמך – to rejoice.
[13] Rav Noach Orlowek.

Beshalach - Graceful Emulation[1]

עָזִּי וְזִמְרָת יָ-הּ, וַיְהִי-לִי לִישׁוּעָה; זֶה אֵ-לִי וְאַנְוֵהוּ, אֱלֹקֵי אָבִי
וַאֲרֹמְמֶנְהוּ.

God's strength and power have been my salvation. This is
my God **וְאַנְוֵהוּ**; the God of my father and I will exalt God.

Exodus 15:2

As their Egyptian oppressors are swallowed up by the sea,
Israel bursts into exultant song. It is a song of victory, a
celebration of freedom and human dignity. The Israelites
had been enslaved for hundreds of years, Moshe and
Aaron had been fighting with Pharaoh for many months,
and now finally the battle was over.

The problem is that even after crossing the sea, the
Israelites are still in the desert. Vanquishing our foes does
not automatically lead to achieving our goals. Israel needs
to move forward to Sinai to receive the Torah, and

---

[1] This essay was co-authored with Rabba Wendy Amsellem.

forward further to the promised land to create their ideal society.

Midrash Tanchuma[2] explains that Moshe had to push Israel to move past the sea. The people wanted to stay where they were, relishing their triumph and collecting the Egyptian baubles they found floating in the water. We can get stuck in a moment of success and forget that the real work has not yet even begun. The Song of the Sea contains advice for how to remember to orient towards our goals.

The word וְאַנְוֵהוּ is interpreted in multiple ways. Talmud Bavli Shabbat 133b explains:

אַבָּא שָׁאוּל אוֹמֵר: ״וְאַנְוֵהוּ״—הֱוֵי דוֹמֶה לוֹ, מָה הוּא חַנּוּן
וְרַחוּם—אַף אַתָּה הֱיֵה חַנּוּן וְרַחוּם

Abba Shaul teaches: "וְאַנְוֵהוּ" means we must strive to be like God – just as God is gracious and merciful, we too must be gracious and merciful.

Rashi adds:

הוי דומה לו—ולשון "אנוהו" אני והוא אעשה עצמי כמותו
לדבק בדרכיו

Be like God—the word "וְאַנְוֵהוּ" is an anagram of אני והוא, I and God. I will make myself like God and do as God does.

---

[2] 16 (Buber).

The mandate to continually strive to be more like God is the antidote for complacency in our current victory. The verse, and the moment, model the shift from being oppressed, and in the opposition, to channeling the freedom and momentum forward.

There is power and energy in fighting for freedom. As long as we are in the opposition, we have a clear goal, but it can be harder to maintain our drive once we are empowered to actually make things better. For human beings, it is difficult to hold focus, but when we strive to be like God, we are always working towards a more perfect existence.

The Talmud[3] teaches that when Pharaoh decreed that all baby boys be killed, the pregnant Israelite women would slip out to the fields to give birth in secret and then leave the babies there. In a lovely description of Divine nurturing, God cares for the babies and provides food and sustenance. When the children grow older, they return home to their parents but they always remember their early encounters with the all-protecting Deity. At the Splitting of the Sea, these children are the first to recognize God, familiar as they are with God's providence. They declare זֶה אֵ-לִי וְאַנְוֵהוּ, "This is my God and I want to be like God," providing protection and sustenance to others.

This is the essence of graceful emulation. We must strive to be like God, using our talents and energy to help others. The little children who are cared for by God grow up to be adults who perceive God and try to be like God in caring

---

[3] Bavli Sotah 11b.

for others. This role is observed by the mystical work, Sefer Yetzirah, which teaches grace/חן is governed by the letter ת, which (added to חן) forms the word חתן/groom. Pirkei D'Rabbi Eliezer compares a groom to a king because both, historically, are the center of attention and have the power to influence all those around them. The letter ת has a numerical value of 400 and relates to the 400 years of enslavement, in which the Israelites' souls, as well as their bodies, were shackled. At the splitting of the sea, the people found physical and spiritual liberation.

The word וְאַנְוֵהוּ can also be related to the Hebrew word נוי, or beauty. Tradition[4] explains that זֶה אֵ-לִי וְאַנְוֵהוּ is accomplished by performing God's commandments in a beautiful way. We should not just acquire any shofar or lulav. Rather, we should be sure to get a beautiful one, and in so doing we beautify our relationship with God. In his work Imrei Gedalia, Rav Gedalia Finkel teaches that an aspect of beautification is making sure that we protect and prevent our actions from falling below an acceptable threshold. This posture requires us to focus on advancing the good and not losing hard earned progress.

Even when we are united in purpose, we can still be waylaid by disagreements over implementation. The Talmud[5] describes this scene right before the sea splits:

דתניא, היה ר"מ אומר: כשעמדו ישראל על הים, היו שבטים
מנצחים זה עם זה, זה אומר אני יורד תחלה לים וזה אומר

---

4 Bavli Shabbat 133b.
5 Bavli Sotah 36b.

אני יורד תחלה לים, קפץ שבטו של בנימין וירד לים תחילה,
. . . והיו שרי יהודה רוגמים אותם

It was taught: R. Meir said: When the Israelites stood by
the Sea of Reeds, the tribes were fighting with one
another. One said, "I will go down first!" The other said,
"I will go down first." The tribe of Benjamin jumped and
descended into the sea first. . . .and the officers of the tribe
of Yehuda threw stones at them.

All of the tribes of Israel recognize that they need to cross
through the sea. When the tribe of Benjamin jumps
forward though, to actually do it, the tribe of Judah does
not commend them. Instead, Judah throws stones at
Benjamin. If we want to work together to accomplish our
goals, we must keep those goals in mind and not be
distracted by arguments over who is being highlighted for
credit.

This is not to say that the identity of change leaders is
irrelevant. Real progress is often determined by who takes
charge. Historically, men have been on the forefront of
social movements because they have had the resources and
social standing to make themselves heard. The
beautification of today's organizing is achieved through
diverse representation and a deep unification of the
collective, ensuring the soul's ascendancy over the
subjugation of gender inequality.

Yisro - Graceful Simplicity

אָנֹכִי יְקֹוָק אֱלֹהֶיךָ, אֲשֶׁר הוֹצֵאתִיךָ מֵאֶרֶץ מִצְרַיִם מִבֵּית עֲבָדִים:

I am Hashem, your God, who took you out of the land of Egypt, from the house of slaves.

Exodus 20:2

The Divine Revelation at Mount Sinai was God's coming out speech. In it, God tells us about God's self. God is everywhere, all of the time, relating to everything in this world in countless ways - and God is One. Indeed, what may be most complicated to grasp about God, is God's utter simplicity.[1]

"I am Hashem your God" is confusing for us. The verse includes two different names for God: Hashem and

---

[1] R' Moshe Chaim Luzzatto's fifth principle about Hashem: "One must further know that Hashem's existence is simple, without any composite or multiplicity. All perfections in their entirety are found within. God in a simple way (שמציאותו יתברך שמו מציאות פשות).

Elokim. One name for God seems to be individualized - Elokecha, "your" God - while the other name sounds absolute.[2] The variations we perceive between these different names of God are a result of God reflecting our diversity back to us in relationships.

It's noteworthy that God introduces God's self in this verse as the God who took us out of Egypt, while at Mount Sinai God presented as "an old man full of mercy."[3] Earlier, at the splitting of the sea, God appeared as a "mighty warrior." Even though the people of Israel perceived God differently, God is in fact One. God explains, "Since I change appearances, do not say that there are two different powers."[4]

God's simplicity continues to be complex for us. It certainly could have been a more powerful claim to simply state: "I am Hashem your God who created the universe." But that is harder for us to relate to. No one was there at the time of Creation, but everyone at Mount Sinai had just witnessed the ten plagues and the splitting of the sea.

In preparation for experiencing the revelation of God at Sinai, the verse testifies, "Israel (singular) encamped there, opposite the mountain," וַיִּחַן-שָׁם יִשְׂרָאֵל, נֶגֶד הָהָר.[5] Rashi explains that Israel is described in the singular to indicate that they were encamped as one person with one heart. To

2 עיין בתפארת ישראל קז.
3 See Rashi.
4 Rashi 20:2.
5 Exodus 19:2.

encamp, וַיִּחַן, uses a language of grace.[6] Gathering the entire nation, unified in purpose and intention is not a small task, and was only made possible because of this attribute of grace. It allowed everyone to see each other's character traits, and not to hate or separate from each other because of differences.[7]

The Divine revelation required a process of relatability: separate and distinct things coming together as one. In truth, we are all made of the same traits, attributes, and characteristics, just blended in unique ways with individualized expressions. Below the surface we all carry similar things, just in different ways, the result of our own life experiences.

We are each a part of the whole of humanity. Nothing is found in the whole except that which is found in the individual.[8] There is a part of each of us in the other. This is true of the commandments as well. For example, there is a mitzvah to honor the Sabbath; and every mitzvah also has an aspect of honor in it. The red heifer is emblematic of an unintelligible commandment; and we also recognize that every mitzvah has aspects beyond our comprehension. "I am Hashem your God" is necessary for it all.

The manifestation of a trait as the dominant expression in a moment doesn't minimize the existence of all of the other attributes that also make us who we are. When we

---

[6] הרבי מוורקה.

[7] כד הקמח.

[8] אין בכלל אלא מה שבפרט.

dismiss people by what we think defines them, we flatten the depth and deny the complexities of God's creations. When we recognize each person as valuable for specifically the constellation of character traits that makes them unique (and different from us), we come closer to perceiving and understanding the total unity of God.

Mishpatim - Graceful Forgiveness

וְאֵלֶּה, הַמִּשְׁפָּטִים, אֲשֶׁר תָּשִׂים, לִפְנֵיהֶם.

And these are the judgments that you shall place before them.

Exodus 21:1

When we ask God for forgiveness, in our daily prayers, we bless God as "the gracious One who pardons abundantly." The Zera Kodesh explains that we need "abundance" because even when we apologize to God for our mistakes, and regret them, our understanding of the impact of our actions is limited. We cannot fathom the full extent of our wrongs, and therefore cannot adequately appreciate what we are asking for in begging for forgiveness.

The Zera Kodesh offers a parable of a simple villager who breaks an ornate window belonging to the king. Not having any understanding of the exorbitant value of the broken window, the villager brings an inferior one to the king as a replacement when asking for forgiveness. The king, compassionate and gracious, accepts the apology and the window, but then shows the villager the process of collecting and adding the precious stones and the exquisite artisanal embellishments required to return the window to its original state. Only then does the villager understand how much damage they really did, and just how forgiving the king was in accepting his inadequate restitution.

This is true in our human relationships as well. It is almost impossible to ever really understand the true depth of hurt and damage we cause another. Even when someone lets us know that our actions caused them pain, our first reaction is often to minimize our role to avoid taking full responsibility. It is perhaps for this reason that the Mishnah,[1] when teaching about damages, deviates from the standard third person language. Instead, it uses a first person point of view, to center the text in one's ownership of one's impact:

"כל שחבתי בשמירתו הכשרתי את נזקו הכשרתי במקצת נזקו חבתי בתשלומי נזקו כהכשר כל נזקו

Anything that I am obligated to safeguard, I am responsible if it becomes damaged. If I facilitated part of the damage it caused, I am liable for payments of restitution for damage it caused, as if I were the one who facilitated the entire damage it caused."

Parshat Mishpatim opens with God telling Moses to "place [the laws] before them." Rashi explains that God was teaching Moses that when it comes to these laws, it is not

---

[1] Bava Kama 9b.

enough to just teach and review until people have memorized them, but rather he must go further and expound on the reasons and explanations until it is clearly presented before them.

The Talmud[2] asks:

כֵּיצַד סֵדֶר מִשְׁנָה?

How was the teaching organized?

The Talmud explains that Moshe taught it four times, and this teaches that students need repetition and need to learn new material four times. Rav Nosson Gestetner explains that the four times is understood as a reference to *pardes*, פרדס, the four levels at which the Torah can be understood. The Mishna is the *p'shat*/פשט, the simple teaching. The other 3 levels in *pardes* (*sod*/סוד, the hidden secrets, *drash*/דרש, homiletics, *remez*/רמז) all allude to the סדר, order.

An essential aspect of understanding the laws of damages is recognizing how deep and profound the effect of our actions can be. In other words: it's not enough to simply teach commandments so that people understand the way to behave. We need to impart with clarity a sense of responsibility and ownership for the hidden, and often traumatic, impact of our actions.

---

[2] Bavli Eruvin 54b.

The word "judgment"/הַמִּשְׁפָּטִים, is understood by the Baal Haturim—the author of the Tur, the precursor to the Code of Jewish Law—as an acronym: הדיין מצווה שיעשה פשרה טרם יעשה משפט, "the adjudicator is obligated to make a compromise before issuing a judgment." When two people are in conflict, and both feel entitled to something, they should each first try to share their experience with the other. When we ask someone for forgiveness, we may be asking them to compromise, and to give something up.

Forgiveness can also allow for a reconciliation that brings people closer together, perhaps even closer than they were before. The Vilna Gaon understands the word *rachamim*/mercy as the tool for forgiveness, and *chein*/grace as the transformation of a negative act into a positive one. The blessing for forgiveness asks God to "Return us in complete repentance before you," understood by the Nefesh HaChaim as "out of love." Saying that we are sorry doesn't undo what happened. However, if we can approach offering an apology from a heart-space, with a deep commitment to understanding how we negatively impacted another, the apology can go a long way to heal the pain of the past and build healthier relationships in the future.

Terumah - Graceful Table

וְשַׂמְתָּ אֶת-הַשֻּׁלְחָן, מִחוּץ לַפָּרֹכֶת, וְאֶת-הַמְּנֹרָה נֹכַח הַשֻּׁלְחָן,
עַל צֶלַע הַמִּשְׁכָּן תֵּימָנָה; וְהַשֻּׁלְחָן–תִּתֵּן, עַל-צֶלַע צָפוֹן.

You shall place the table outside of the dividing curtain,
and the menorah opposite the table on the southern side
of the tabernacle and the table you shall place on the
northern side.

Exodus 26:35

"Let them build for me a tabernacle and I will dwell
among them." God's command at the start of Parshat
Terumah is famously understood as "I will dwell in each
and every one of you." Why is it necessary then to build
God a physical space, for the resting of the Divine
Presence, if God dwells within us all?

To better understand the purpose of the tabernacle and
how it allowed us to come closer to God, particularly
through offerings (the Hebrew word *korban*/offering
comes from the root meaning "to draw close"), it is

helpful to see how we have responded to our current lack of a physical dwelling place for God.

"The altar, three cubits high…This is the table that is before the Lord".[1] The prophet starts with "altar" and ends with "table." The Talmud explains the connection: "When the Temple is standing, the altar atones for a person; now (that the Temple has been destroyed), it is a person's table that atones for them."

It is for this reason that many have salt on our tables, like the salt that was part of the offerings. It's also for this reason that many remove, or cover, any knives before the Grace After Meals. The Mechilta understands the prohibition[2] of using hewn stones for an altar because "[the altar] was created to lengthen a person's life, and iron was created to shorten a person's life." Since the altar should not have cutting implements on it, there is a tradition to remove them from our tables as well.

The Talmud[3] teaches, "whoever extends their table, their life is extended." The Rabbis understand this blessing to come when we are prepared to help a person experiencing food insecurity and, more broadly, inviting guests to come together over food.

On the verse, "Cedars are the beams of our house, Cypresses the rafters,"[4] the Gra comments that, although

---

[1] Ezekiel 41:22.
[2] Exodus 20:22.
[3] Bavli Berachot 54b.
[4] Song of Songs 1:17.

God dwells among each of us, we needed a singular place to gather and unify all of our individual hearts together. That place was the tabernacle, which was built by the collective, through individual contributions of the heart. God's primary resting place is determined by our hearts coming together as one, whether at the giving of the Torah or in the Temple.

Jerusalem is described by King David as "a city that is united together,"[5] and is understood by the Jerusalem Talmud as "The city that brings everyone to friendship." It is perhaps for this reason that we are taught that the Temple was destroyed because of blatant hatred. Destruction is simply the consequence of division and lack of caring for each other.

Being able to come together around the same table is an act of atonement for separation, and a restoration of the closeness that we once had with God and each other. That is why it is so essential to bring the right intentions to the table.

In Hebrew, the word for table, שלחן/shulchan, is parsed by the Ben Ish Chai as של חן/shel chein/of grace. "Only when it is filled with grace will it atone," and bring people together. We find the power of the evil opposition alluded to in the word as well. In Psalm 23, King David says, "You prepare a table for me before my enemies." The word "שלחן/table" also contains the word "נחש/snake," an

---

5 Psalms 122:3.

allusion to the potential for food to be misused and cause a separation between people and God.

After nearly a year of being physically apart from each other in community, we find ourselves in Adar/אדר which is understood as living together as one: א-דר. This coming week we will celebrate Purim, which is a holiday of tremendous "unity and togetherness." Purim is also, though, the only holiday that is not observed by all Jews on the same day, as those in unwalled cities celebrate on the 14th of Adar and those in walled cities celebrate on the 15th of Adar. Being apart or different doesn't mean that we are not connected, as long as we are able to see the holiness of the Divine in each and every one of us.

Tetzaveh - Graceful Companionship

וְאַתָּה תְּצַוֶּה אֶת-בְּנֵי יִשְׂרָאֵל, וְיִקְחוּ אֵלֶיךָ שֶׁמֶן זַיִת זָךְ כָּתִית—
לַמָּאוֹר: לְהַעֲלֹת נֵר, תָּמִיד.

And you will command the Children of Israel that they
shall take for you clear olive oil, crushed, for illumination,
to light a lamp continually.

Exodus 27:20

Although God is speaking to Moses, Moses is addressed as
"you." Not only is Moses's name omitted from the first
verse of the Torah portion, his name is not mentioned in it
at all! The Baal Haturim understands this phenomenon as
a fulfillment of Moses's request from God that he be
erased from the Torah if God wouldn't forgive the Jews
for the sin of the Golden Calf.[1]

Perhaps the reason why this location is chosen for Moses's
perceived absence is because "to light a lamp continually"

---

[1] Exodus 32:32.

is a reference to learning Torah.[2] As King Solomon[3] teaches, "a commandment is a lamp, and the Torah is light." Moses, by removing himself here, is exemplifying the teaching: "The matters of Torah do not endure except in one who considers himself as if they are nothing."[4]

The word "erased/מח," is also an allusion to the מח, 48, ways of acquiring the wisdom[5] of the Torah, and is necessary in forming the word "wise," חכם. True knowledge leaves an impression and connects us to God. The Talmud teaches, "One who walks along the way without having someone to accompany them should occupy themselves with words of Torah, as it is stated (with regard to words of Torah): 'For they shall be a chaplet of חן, grace, to your head, and chains around your neck.'"[6]

"Tetzaveh" is a language of commandment, and also of connectivity. When we relate to God through the learning of Torah, then it accompanies us on our journey. It's noteworthy that the Talmud chooses to highlight this benefit of Torah study when one is alone. We are taught that if two people are together and do not speak words of Torah, then it is a meeting of scoffers.[7] There is a unique,

---

[2] L'horos Nosson.
[3] Proverbs 6:23.
[4] Bavli Sotah 21b.
[5] Avos 6:6.
[6] Proverbs 1:9 and Sotah 46b.
[7] Pirkei Avos 3:2.

and perhaps deeper, connection when we are guided by those who are not physically in our presence.

Our attachments affect and influence us. The Talmud[8] declares, "Jacob our father never died." The Rabbis challenge this claim by quoting the scriptures that mention his funeral. The teaching is then clarified by stating, "Just as his descendants are alive, so too is he still alive." When we affect another, their related actions are also an extension of our impact.

Yocheved, Moses's mother, is credited by the *medrash* with giving birth to 600,000 children because of the role her son played in leading the nation to Mount Sinai. This connection between generations is especially true for the learning of Torah.

Reish Lakish[9] says: "Anyone who occupies themselves with Torah at night, the Holy One, Blessed be God, extends a thread of kindness over them by day, as it is stated: 'By day, the Lord will command God's kindness, and in the night God's song shall be with me.'"[10] Rashi explains this Divine extension of kindness as "the person presenting with grace to others."

We must strive to be *talmidei chachamim*, students and practitioners of wisdom. When we allow God's wisdom to guide our path in life, we always travel with great company.

---

[8] Bavli Taanis 5b.
[9] Bavli Avodah Zarah 3b.
[10] Psalms 42:9.

Ki Sisa - Graceful Optimism

וַיִּשְׁמַע הָעָם, אֶת-הַדָּבָר הָרָע הַזֶּה--וַיִּתְאַבָּלוּ; וְלֹא-שָׁתוּ אִישׁ
עֶדְיוֹ, עָלָיו.

The people heard this bad tiding and they mourned; and
they, each man, did not put on his crown.

Exodus 33:4

When God created this world, it was filled with hope,
possibilities, and aspirations. On the sixth day of creation
God said וַיַּרְא אֱלֹהִים אֶת-כָּל-אֲשֶׁר עָשָׂה וְהִנֵּה-טוֹב מְאֹד וַיְהִי-
עֶרֶב וַיְהִי-בֹקֶר יוֹם הַשִּׁשִּׁי. "And God saw all that God had
made, and found it very good. And there was evening and
there was morning, the sixth day."[1] At that moment,
according to the *medrash*, God declared, "I wish that there
would always be as much grace before me as there is
now." The grace that God is referring to here is the grace

---

[1] Genesis 1:31.

85

that is found when the desire for evil is converted to good and then becomes "very good/*tov meod*."

This grace was ultimately achieved again at Mount Sinai, with the giving of the Torah. Even the angel of death was banished[2] on the sixth day of Sivan. This moment was so essential to the purpose of this world that the Rabbis[3] read "The sixth day," in Genesis, as the acceptance of the Torah by Israel on the sixth day of Sivan as a condition for the world's continued existence.

The Talmud explains that when we said, "We will do and we will listen," angels descended and wove two crowns upon our heads. Tragically this was undone with the sin of the golden calf, which the people requested when it appeared to them that Moshe was delayed in returning from the mountain.[4] The word for delayed, בשֵׁשׁ, is understood[5] as "with the sixth" hour of the day, and it was at that moment that we lost our crowns.

Recanti[6] explains that חֵן/*chein*/grace is a language of "crown," as in Proverbs 1:9, when the traditions of parents are described as: "They are a graceful crown upon your head." It is not coincidental that we find the word "grace" six times in this *parsha* as the remedy for our miscalculation.

---

[2] Bavli Eruvin 54a.
[3] Bavli Shabbos 88a.
[4] Exodus 32:1.
[5] Bavli Shabbos 89a.
[6] Vayeitzei.

God wanted to create this world exclusively through the strict attribute of judgment, but saw that a world created in such a way wouldn't last, so God made a partnership with mercy. The purpose of mercy, in this arrangement, is to create a path back to the ideal space, free from negative judgment. Ups and downs are certainly part of life, and the true test of our faith is what we do when we find ourselves in the lower spots.

Rashi explains that after the sin of the golden calf, the Jewish people mourned the loss of their crowns. R' Moses Feinstein[7] understands their grief as coming from a mistaken sense of hopelessness. They felt that their distance from God was permanent, and that they would never be able to restore the glory of their former closeness. The Shach explains[8] "Moshe took" meaning that he returned the crowns to them on *erev shabbos*.

We are not static; we have the capacity to change for good. King David wrote,[9] "Who may ascend the mountain of the Lord? Who may stand in God's holy place?" Coming down from a mountain doesn't mean we can't still stand in a holy place.

The numerical value of the word חן/*chein*/grace is 58. The six times that "חן" appears in this week's Torah reading add up to 348, the value of the word שמח/happy. Making amends for our mistakes is a mitzvah, and we are meant to

---

[7] Drash Moshe.

[8] 33:7.

[9] Psalms 24:3.

serve God with joy. Our ability to correct the missteps of the past, and our faith in God's desire for us to be imbued with grace, is a source of light and gladness even in dark and troubled times.

Vayakhel - Graceful Expansion

וַיָּבֹאוּ, כָּל-אִישׁ אֲשֶׁר-נְשָׂאוֹ לִבּוֹ; וְכֹל אֲשֶׁר נָדְבָה רוּחוֹ אֹתוֹ, הֵבִיאוּ אֶת-תְּרוּמַת יְהוָה לִמְלֶאכֶת אֹהֶל מוֹעֵד וּלְכָל-עֲבֹדָתוֹ, וּלְבִגְדֵי, הַקֹּדֶשׁ.

Everyone whose heart was inspired came; and everyone whose spirit moved them brought the portion of Hashem for the work of the Tent of Meeting, and for all its labor and for the holy garments.

Exodus 35:21

Moshe gathers *all* of the assembly[1] - כל - in order to give instructions to guide the construction of the Tabernacle. We find the same word, "כל", deployed three times in this verse. Twice it is modified by motivations: "*all* whose heart was inspired," and "*all* whose spirit was moved". The

---

[1] Exodus 35:1.

commentators[2] seek to understand the difference between these two categories of people.

One interpretation[3] is that there are actually two distinct modalities of giving. One is when a person gives willingly, according to their own ability and resources; one whose spirit moves them. The higher level, however, is when a person's heart is so inspired that it is "נשאו," elevated and raised above the natural limits and constraints of what otherwise would be the best that they could do. It is the shift from the giving of a thing, to being that which is given.[4]

To better understand this concept, it is essential to explore its context in the building of the Tabernacle, or in Hebrew, *mishkan*/משכן.[5] This language is similar to that of משכון— a deposit or collateral. Just as our souls are placed temporarily in our bodies, the Tabernacle was a temporary dwelling place for the Divine Presence. The "מלאכה," or the different types of labor/work necessary to create the Tabernacle, has the same etymology as "מלאך" angel. This is because the exclusive identity of any angel sent on a task, is that task itself. The offerings of the *mishkan* are meant to model how we should more broadly see the offerings of our daily living - to fill the space of the mundane with the holiness of the Divine.

---

[2] See Ramban.
[3] Ohr Hachaim.
[4] L'Horos Nosson.
[5] Toras HaRemez.

The converse perhaps better articulates this dynamic. A desecration of God's name is known as a *chillul Hashem*/חילול ה'[6], and the Talmud[6] declares that it is such a grave transgression that not even repentance or Yom Kippur atones for it. It is a word of void - חל - that whatever the negative action was, it was not inspired or influenced by the Divine Will. Such an incident could only have happened when a person was acting in a way that was devoid of the consciousness of the Divine Presence.

By contrast, "commandment/מצוה" and "obligation/חובה" are expressions of connectivity and affection: צוותא and חיבה. They represent expectations in our relationship with God, but don't at all limit the opportunities we have to become closer. When a person wants and desires for more involvement in, and greater understanding of, their intended contributions to this world, they are granted additional access. This is what King Somolom meant[7] when he wrote: "give to the wise and they will become even wiser."[8] It wasn't natural talent that built the Tabernacle, but the human will to transcend the physical boundaries of knowledge, receiving Divine Inspiration.[9]

The *mishkan* was an immersive experience demonstrating that our ultimate potential can only be attained when we go all in. It is perhaps for this reason that this *parsha,*

---

[6] Bavli Yoma 86a.
[7] Midrash Rabbah 50:2.
[8] Proverbs 9:9.
[9] Ramban 31:2 and see Chronicles 2 17:6.

"ויקהל," has the same numerical value as "מקוה," a ritual body of water that requires an absolute and total immersion in it. If even one hair sticks out of the water, the immersion is considered invalid.

It is this wholeness that creates holiness. Whether it is the totality of the nation gathering to hear the complete Torah, which if even one letter is missing from is invaild, or the full focus of an individual's heart wanting to connect their entire selves to God; this is a reflection of the oneness of the Divine. We normally think about tithing as giving a part, literally a tenth, of the whole. Here, however, the portion that we are offering is our undivided desire to be constantly living with God.

The Prophet Zechariah[10] tells of a time when God will "pour on us a spirit of grace," and the Rabbis[11] understand this to be in response to our wanting to be in God's grace. Aspiring to do the right thing extends the grace so that it spills over us. Additionally, the mystics[12] observe the equity that is achieved when people are occupied with directing their unique offerings which could never be duplicated by another.

We can't do more than our best, but tradition[13] teaches that when we do all that we are able, we will find that God has elevated us to a higher place with greater abilities still to be utilized. Just like a farmer toils in the field, but then

---

[10] Zechariah 12:10.
[11] See Metzudat Dovid.
[12] Eitz Hadas Tov.
[13] Chovas Halvavos Chesbon Hanefesh 3:21.

God causes the plants to grow, our investments also sprout above and beyond, allowing us to be a sanctuary for the Divine.

Pekudei - Graceful Recognition

וַיַּרְא מֹשֶׁה אֶת-כָּל-הַמְּלָאכָה, וְהִנֵּה עָשׂוּ אֹתָהּ--כַּאֲשֶׁר צִוָּה
יְקוָק, כֵּן עָשׂוּ; וַיְבָרֶךְ אֹתָם, מֹשֶׁה.

Moses saw all of the work and behold! They had done it as
Hashem had commanded, so had they done; and Moses
blessed them.

Exodus 39:43

When we appreciate something, we increase its value. We
might begin by recognizing its goodness, and then expand
to include the deeper consequences of it. For example, if
one is thirsty and someone provides water to drink, the
water tastes good and one is grateful for it. The *Bilvavi
Mishkan Evneh* explains, though, that the water is only the
vessel that contains the goodness, an act of care from one
person to another, not the goodness itself. This is true of
the entire creation narrative, where God declares after the
completion of each day's work, "כי טוב," and it was good;

that the goodness exists within creation - not just that the creation is a good creation.[1]

The *medrash* claims that the "work" that Moshe saw was actually this work of creation, and that the verse comes to equate the construction of the Tabernacle to the formation of the world. Reviewing the work of building the Tabernacle is similar to noticing God's creation of the world in that, in both cases, we need to revisit what we have already gotten accustomed to, and not take it for granted. The Belzer Rebbe[2] saw this reflected in the repetition of "and so they did." He writes that the first time it appears in the verse, is for the actual completion of the *mishkan,* and the second time is to re-experience it with greater intentionality and holiness.

וְהִנֵּה, "Behold," represents seeing something as if you are pointing at it with a finger.[3] Moshe was able to see both the hidden and revealed creations simultaneously, and immediately responded with a blessing. This paradox is emblematic of all things holy:[4] the body is revealed while the soul is concealed. Moshe validates the true depth of our beauty, that we are worthy of being the sanctuaries in which the Divine Presence literally dwells[5] by saying "you are the blessing."

---

[1] See Bilvavi Mishkan Evneh on chapter eight of Path of the Just.
[2] Rabbi Yissacar Dov.
[3] Bris Olam.
[4] Bais Aharon.
[5] Rav Tov.

The *medrash*[6] informs us that the words of the blessing were from Psalms[7]:

וִיהִי נֹעַם אֲדֹנָי אֱלֹקֵינוּ עָלֵינוּ וּמַעֲשֵׂה יָדֵינוּ כּוֹנְנָה
עָלֵינוּ וּמַעֲשֵׂה יָדֵינוּ כּוֹנְנֵהוּ:

May the pleasantness of the Lord our God
be upon us; our handiwork, establish for us,
our handiwork, establish it.

In the mystical work of the Zohar,[8] we find the concept that God's name י-ה-ו-ה is placed on the head of a person, and that it arouses in a person the awareness of God. The Shla HaKodesh[9] uses this teaching to explain,[10] " שׁוִּיתִי י"י לְנגדי תמיד" as "I have set God before me always," and renders "ואתם הדבקים בי"/And you shall cleave to God," as actually cleaving to the Divine Presence which is engraved on one's head. He argues that this process creates *chein*/grace. The Talmud[11] teaches: כָּל אָדָם שֶׁיֵּשׁ עָלָיו חֵן, בְּיָדוּעַ שֶׁהוּא יְרֵא שָׁמַיִם, anyone who has on them grace, it is known that they have an awareness of God.

The Ari z"l[12] extends this idea to the phrase ברוך כבוד י"י ממקומו, and observes that the Hebrew word for "grace" has the same numerical value as God's glory, כבוד י"י

---

[6] Bamidbar Rabbah 2:19.

[7] 90:17.

הזוהר פרשת נשא. [8]

[9] Vavei HaAmudim 15.

[10] Psalms 16:8.

[11] Bavli Sukkah 49b.

[12] Kanfie Yona.

בגימטריא חן.[13] Grace is a reflection of the consciousness of seeing the glory of God in all places.

This blessing is the blessing that includes all other blessings.[14] Revealing the hidden goodness exposes the perceived difficulty as simply the container for the good, and then the hardship is minimized and reduced. The ability to experience the pleasantness of effort, particularly when it is laborious, enhances the pleasure of living, without retreating from the work that still needs to be done.

Hakaras hatov, having gratitude, means developing the skills to recognize the good. Shabbat is a unique time for this exercise, because we shift from the externality of the physical world to welcoming the spiritual when we allow the soul to come out. This is one of the interpretations of the widespread custom to sing "Shalom Aleichem" on the night of Shabbat: we are re-introducing ourselves to the more authentic, spiritual version of ourselves.

It is also among the reasons that the building of the *mishkan* was suspended for Shabbat. The desired intimacy of the *mishkan*, a heavenly abode on earth, can be achieved through the additional soul on Shabbat - transporting us to a dimension that is *mein olam haba,* from the source of the supernal.

---

[13] With the 26 from God's name.
[14] R' Pinchas page 417.

Perhaps this is the intention of the blessing that Moses offers: We know that God is good, and we yearn to have that goodness manifested in our actions in this world so that they parallel the goodness above. In that way, identifying goodness is an exploration of Godliness.

Sefer Vayikra

Vayikra - Graceful Offerings

וְאִם־מִן־הָעוֹף עֹלָה קָרְבָּנוֹ, לַיהוָה: וְהִקְרִיב מִן־הַתֹּרִים, אוֹ מִן־בְּנֵי הַיּוֹנָה—אֶת־קָרְבָּנוֹ.

If one's offering to Hashem is an *olah* offering from the fowl, one should bring their offering from the turtledoves or from the young doves.

Vayikra 1:14

When God introduces God's self to Moses at the burning bush,[1] God says: "Do not come closer. Remove your sandals from your feet, for the place on which you stand is holy ground." At Mount Sinai, when God reveals God's self to the world, it is also amidst fire, and again we are warned to make borders and not approach the mountain.[2] The main purpose of the Torah is to guide us in coming closer to God. This models a healthy relationship in which

---

[1] Exodus 3:5.
[2] Exodus 19:12.

each party defines what the appropriate closeness is for themselves, which then informs the available proximity that the other is invited to approach.

The offerings, *korbanos* in Hebrew, literally means acts of closeness, and are a representation of self sacrifice. However, not all acts of self sacrifice bring us closer to the Divine, or to each other. It is necessary to be able to discern which are the healthy and holy pleasures that we are meant to pursue—those that elevate all involved and transcend physical limitations into spiritual spaces. We need to take care not to cross dangerous lines of consumption and debasement, while also avoiding asceticism.

The first chapter of Vayikra discusses bird sacrifices. "From the turtle doves," מן התורים/*min hatorim*, is understood as an allusion to two Torahs, the oral and the written.[3] There is often a vast space between what the text says and what it actually means. God tells us that investing and toiling in the process of understanding the Divine Will, through Torah study, brings us closer to God. Perhaps for this reason, the Talmud teaches[4] that the study of Torah is greater than the offering of the sacrifices.

Hillel had 80 principal students, the greatest of whom was Yonatan ben Uzziel. The story is told[5] that when Yonatan ben Uzziel sat and learned Torah, any bird that would fly

---

[3] Rabbeinu Efrayim.
[4] Bavli Eruvin 63b.
[5] Bavli Sukkah 28a.

over his head would be incinerated. Tosafot explains that his teachings were comparable to the giving of Torah, which was done with fire. Another Medieval commentary, R' Chananel, explains that the Divine Presence was there, and therefore the space was designated as sacred.

Yonatan ben Uzziel is also the author of the classic *targum*, translation of the holy texts, known by his name. The Minchas Elazar posits that the act of translation, by its nature, is to bring outsiders in by granting access to otherwise guarded spaces. For this reason, it was necessary to add an additional layer of protection and to mark the contours of this space with fire.

The Torah is also referred to as *derech*/a "path,"[6] because it informs how we are meant to travel and navigate this world. In Sotah 49a we are warned that if two Torah scholars are walking along the way/*derech* and there are no words of Torah between them, then they are deserving of being burned in fire. The Ben Yehoyada explains this teaching by quoting the Prophet Jeremiah[7] saying that Torah is also called אש/*aish*/fire. He continues that those who learn Torah generate חן/*chein*/grace, and observes that the combined numerical value of fire and grace, 301+58, equals שטן, or 359/Satan, a force that was appointed to distract us from God. "Therefore, two scholars who are traveling on a dangerous path, and are not learning Torah to combat the evil opposition, are then

[6] Exodus 18:20.
[7] 23:29.

101

worthy of being consumed by the fire of Satan," instead of being led by the light of Torah.

It is the way of the evil inclination to falsely present the bad as good, like "stolen waters are sweet."[8] Our response, the Rabbis teach[9] is to "pull it into the study hall," quoting again from Jeremiah: "Is not My word like fire, says the Lord?". Through the study of Torah we are able to both connect to the source of all truth and also achieve the ultimate pleasure, coming closer to God through respectfully engaging with each other.

---

[8] Proverbs 9:17.
[9] Bavli Kiddushin 30b.

Tzav - Graceful Humility

וְלָבַשׁ הַכֹּהֵן מִדּוֹ בַד וּמִכְנְסֵי בַד יִלְבַּשׁ עַל בְּשָׂרוֹ וְהֵרִים אֶת הַדֶּשֶׁן אֲשֶׁר תֹּאכַל הָאֵשׁ אֶת הָעֹלָה עַל הַמִּזְבֵּחַ וְשָׂמוֹ אֵצֶל הַמִּזְבֵּחַ.

The priest shall dress in his fitted linen garment, with linen breeches next to his body; and he shall take up the ashes to which the fire has reduced the burnt offering on the altar and place them beside the altar.

Leviticus 6:3

The early mystical work Sefer Yetzirah[1] divides the 22 letters of the Hebrew alphabet into three groups: the three mothers, seven doubles, and twelve elementals. בג"ד כפר"ת are the seven letters that can hold a *dagash*/dot, rendering the capability for a "double" sound—either hard or soft. These seven letters individually correspond to the seven days of the week, but as a group, they form the phrase that can be translated as "garment of atonement."

---

[1] Chapter 1:2.

It is only after Adam and Eve sin that they realize that they are naked, and this creates the need for clothing.[2]

When the Kohen performed the holy work of removing the ashes, his clothing needed to fit just right. This is alluded to in the Hebrew word used to describe his tunic, "מדו," which also means "measured."[3] "*Mido*," his "measurement," can also refer to the Kohen's character trait. It is important that while the Kohen wears his measured garment he has the proper intention to conduct the service with humility and self awareness. It is perhaps for this reason that the Talmud[4] asks: Why was the passage in the Torah discussing the priestly vestments juxtaposed to the passage discussing offerings? To tell you that just as offerings atone, so too the priestly vestments atone.

On a deeper level, the Rabbis connect the need for properly fitting clothes to the second condition of the verse, יִלְבַּשׁ עַל-בְּשָׂרוֹ—that there can't be anything separating the garment and oneself,[5] to teach that the person must also be fit, or worthy, to wear the clothing.[6] Our contributions in Divine service must be a reflection of our inner holiness, expressed without impure motivations that separate us from the source of our holiness.

On a superficial plane, removing the ashes of what was left over from the burnt sacrifice might have been seen as a

---

[2] Genesis 3:7.
[3] Bavli Zevachim 35a.
[4] Bavli Arachin 16a.
[5] Bavli Zevachim 19a.
[6] See Lehoros Nasson.

less than glorious job. The Chovos Halevavos[7] explains that the root of this mitzvah is that it keeps the Kohen humble, and reminds us that our worth isn't dependent on our wisdom or wealth, but that true honor comes with service, from love and joy.[8]

During the Musaf service on Yom Kippur, we compare the Kohen[9] to the "face of the groom."[10] We also find a parallel of similar language about atonement in the Jerusalem Talmud:[11] "All of a groom's sins are forgiven.".

All sins, like the original sin, have their root in aspects of arrogance.[12] The response in the Garden of Eden, of blaming the snake for deceiving us—הִשִּׁיאָנִי—alludes to this truth, containing "there is I/יש אני."[13] Another truth that the Talmud teaches[14] is: כל אדם שיש בו גסות הרוח אמר הקב"ה אין אני והוא יכולין לדור בעולם, "whoever is haughty, God says 'You and I can't co-occupy space'."

By contrast, King Solomon taught:[15] "to the humble God gives grace. This form of grace is not a reward for being humble, but rather a consequence of being in this kind of

---

[7] Gate of Humility.
[8] Tam V'das.
[9] See Menachos 110a that those who study the laws of the offerings are like those who offer them.
[10] Also see Recanti who compares Aron to a groom under his chuppah.
[11] Bavli Bekurim 3:3.
[12] See Lechach V'Halebuv.
[13] Ravid on Sefer Yetzirah.
[14] Bavli Sotah 5a.
[15] Proverbs 3:34.

proximity with God.[16] It is not limited to a relationship with God, but has an expansive influence on interpersonal dynamics as well.

The Chidushei Harim explains that grace comes from knowing that one is not entitled. In that space of gratitude, for the kindness that God has bestowed, grace is given. When the letter ת, corresponding to *shabbos*, properly governs over *chein*, forming חתן/groom, the restoration of creation is achieved, as we find in the blessing said under the *chupah*: "Like in the garden, before the sin."

---

[16] Alshich.

Shemini - Graceful Shame

וַתֵּצֵא אֵשׁ, מִלִּפְנֵי יְהוָה, וַתֹּאכַל עַל-הַמִּזְבֵּחַ, אֶת-הָעֹלָה וְאֶת-
הַחֲלָבִים; וַיַּרְא כָּל-הָעָם וַיָּרֹנּוּ, וַיִּפְּלוּ עַל-פְּנֵיהֶם.

A fire went forth from before Hashem and consumed
from the altar, the olah offering, and the fats; the people
saw and they praised and fell upon their faces.

Vayikra 9:24

Making mistakes, and learning from them, is part of life.
One of the greatest indicators that we have really begun to
internalize a new lesson is a deep feeling of
disappointment and embarrassment that we didn't realize
this particular truth earlier, and that we were ever capable
of making the mistake at all.

This can be a shameful experience that tries to burden us
with negativity that can inhibit growth and change. There
is another holy variety of shame called *busha*/בושה. It
propels us towards a more sensitive version of ourselves
that just can't imagine making that mistake ever again. We

are simply no longer that person and wouldn't ever want to be in the future.

This movement, of coming closer to the ideal, is the act of offerings/*korbanot* (the word comes from a root meaning "to come closer"). Rebbe Yehoshua ben Levi taught[1] that the greatness of being of broken/humble spirits "is as if one has offered all of the sacrifices."

The parable is given of a beloved prince, who one day rebels and acts inappropriately towards his father, the king. As the king deliberates over the correct response, and overcomes his own anger and disappointment with his son, he decides that rather than punishing him directly, he will instead advance the prince's place in the kingdom and afford him even more honor and glory. When the son hears about this generosity, aware in his heart that he truly behaved poorly to his father, he is overcome with *busha* over his immaturity and can't even show his face at the dinner in his honor until he properly apologizes.

After the sin of the Golden Calf, God acted towards the Jewish people with unending love. God so wanted to dwell among the people and bestow goodness that folks were overcome with, and needed to cover their faces in, humility. *Rina*, the Hebrew word used here, is a unique language of praise in that it expresses a mixture of happiness and sadness.[2]

---

[1] Bavli Sotah 5b.
[2] Rav Tov.

Toras Kohanim says that when the fire descended and consumed the offerings the Jewish people declared:[3] "Sing joyfully, righteous strugglers, because of HaShem." It is specifically with "Hashem," the attribute of mercy, that one can approach God from a place of regret, and pain of the past, with gratitude for the opportunity to commit to a different future.

However, the order of the verse is a little strange. Why are the Jewish people praising God before they fall on their faces? If they were really overcome with embarrassment, how did they first sing out before they processed the emotional component?

The Zohar[4] teaches that we don't offer the sacrifices towards the strict attribute of judgment, associated with God's name *Elokim*, but to the *Shem Havayah*, the Tetragrammaton. When spelled out יו"ד-ה"י-ו"ו-ה"י, it has the same numerical value as מזבח, the altar, and with the word[5] itself, each equal חן/grace.

In the mystical tradition,[6] God's foundation of grace was revealed through this exchange on the altar and is hinted to in the Talmud's teaching,[7] that a place/*Makom*—the Omnipresent—is graceful to its inhabitants.

---

[3] Psalms 33:1.
[4] Mishpatim 108a.

עד בכלל. [5]

[6] Bris Kahunas Olam.
[7] Bavli Sotah 47a.

Perhaps it is the compassion of the place where we are, wherever that may be in the moment, recognizing that God is patiently there with us, that stirs us to be vocal about our relationship with God and to give thanks. What follows may be less about a reflection of the past mistake, but more of an attitude towards our future state of being.

After the Ten Commandments were given at Mount Sinai, Moshe told the people: "Be not afraid; for God has come only in order to test you, and in order that the fear of God may be on your faces, so that you do not go astray."[8] The Talmud[9] quotes this verse and declares "זו בושה," "this is shame," and posits: "It is a good quality in a person that they are capable of experiencing shame. Others say: Any person who feels shame will not quickly sin."

Learning more about the way we impact others, through simply being ourselves, is often a painful realization. It can potentially fuel insecurities about being good enough or worthy of being in relationships with others. The Torah teaches us to reject and replace those thoughts of shame with a commitment to a healthier being. It takes faith and a deep desire for self-improvement to explore the next lesson we didn't yet know we needed to learn.

[8] Exodus 20:17.
[9] Bavli Nedarim 20a.

Tazria - Graceful Rebuke

אָדָם, כִּי-יִהְיֶה בְעוֹר-בְּשָׂרוֹ שְׂאֵת אוֹ-סַפַּחַת אוֹ בַהֶרֶת, וְהָיָה בְעוֹר-בְּשָׂרוֹ, לְנֶגַע צָרָעַת–וְהוּבָא אֶל-אַהֲרֹן הַכֹּהֵן, אוֹ אֶל-אַחַד מִבָּנָיו הַכֹּהֲנִים.

If a person will have on their skin of their flesh, a seis, or a sapachas, or a baheres, and it will become a tzaras affliction on the skin of their flesh, they should be brought to Aaron the Kohen, or to one of his sons the Kohanim.

Leviticus 13:2

It is too easy to judge others, even though we know how hard it is to ever really understand what another person is feeling or going through. Indeed, it is often far simpler to recognize an imperfection in someone else than to notice that same flaw in ourselves. If we are so good at observing the failures of others, why is it so difficult for us to see them in ourselves?

Tradition teaches a concept of being *nogea b'davar*, being too close to a matter to maintain objectivity. As an example, one can not act as a judge for a family member.

111

The phrase *nogea b'davar* shares a linguistic root with the word "*nega*," or skin affliction. The Midrash Tanchuma suggests that the word also hints to the causes of the affliction, having their source in crossing the appropriate boundaries of another. As part of the healing process, it is therefore required that "they should be brought" by another person.

Rabbi Yosei ben Zimra additionally taught that anyone who speaks *lashon hara*, malicious speech, will contract this skin ailment. The Talmud[1] teaches, "All of the attributes of God are dispensed measure for measure." Why is this skin ailment an appropriate punishment for gossip?

A person who gossips exposes the flaws of another to public ridicule. As a result, the gossiper is punished by having their own flaws manifest as an external skin disease readily seen by any onlooker.

Instead of speaking badly about someone, the Torah expects us to speak to them. It is not pleasant to receive input that asks us to modify our actions. Yet such a rebuke is the consequence and counterbalance to our own lack of awareness. If we could receive the memo internally, then we wouldn't need another to deliver it.

The Talmud extols the individual who appreciates this type of feedback. Rebbe taught: "A person should love admonition; for as long as it exists in the world, pleasantries come with goodness and blessing and evil is

---

[1] Bavli Sanhedrin 90a.

removed from the world." And R' Yochanan added: "Anyone who rebukes their friends, with the right intentions, merits a portion of the Divine and even more so a cord of grace is extended on them, as it says in Proverbs: 'One who reproves someone will later find grace.'"[2]

The Malbim explains that even though it is the way of the world that people initially prefer to avoid receiving negative feedback, after time, the natural consequences of the "flawed perspective" catch up to a person and then, in the end, they really value the corrective support. It is for this reason that the verse emphasizes "later." So too in the case of the *metzora, the person with the skin ailment*. They need to be brought to the Kohen because they are reluctant to hear the truth about themselves that this affliction will confirm.

In the Vilna Gaon's commentary on the Bible, he explains the prefix "to" in "לנגע" as the Torah's way of teaching us that those around this afflicted individual are aware of the discomfort caused to them, and they are pained in observing it. When we have an insight into the character traits of another, that sensitive information can be used to encourage that person to talk more openly about the motivations and intentions, or it could be the portal into something hurtful, God forbid. The Gra writes that gracefulness is manifested in the awareness that someone

---

[2] Proverbs 28:24.

113

cared enough to take the time, and the chance, to share a heart-centered perspective.

This *parsha* of *negyim* invites us to reflect when we see something in another that doesn't land so well for us— perhaps something similar exists in ourselves. Having something "seen" by someone else helps us have a more accurate vision of ourselves. Rabbi Jacob said: This world is like a vestibule before the world to come; prepare yourself in the vestibule, so that you may enter the banqueting-hall.[3] Rashi explains that people are already dressed and ready for the party by the time they arrive; they just need to make minor adjustments to their hair or clothes before they formally present themselves. We all want to be the best versions of ourselves, and help others do the same, but that requires willingness to see the work that still needs to be done and engage in the process.

---

[3] Pirkei Avos 4:16.

Metzora - Graceful Determination

וְיָצָא, הַכֹּהֵן, אֶל-מִחוּץ, לַמַּחֲנֶה; וְרָאָה, הַכֹּהֵן, וְהִנֵּה נִרְפָּא נֶגַע-הַצָּרַעַת, מִן-הַצָּרוּעַ.

The Kohen shall go out to the outside of the camp; the Kohen shall look, and behold, the *tzara'as* affliction had been healed from the *metzora*.

Leviticus 14:3

It is healthy to want to be desired, and it doesn't feel good to be rejected. When a leper is sent out of the community, it might be easier for them to just walk away entirely. It can take a lot of courage and risk to try to gain acceptance again, and even more effort to change the way that one is perceived by others. Ideally, the *metzora*, the leper, uses the time apart to reflect on, and heal from, the natural outcome of their inappropriate use of speech.

The verse frames the confirmation of healing in an odd way. It could have simply said that the person was healed.

Why does it unnecessarily repeat the ailment?[1] One approach is to understand the period of separation not as a punishment, but as a consequence of being temporarily incompatible with communal living. The verse goes out of its way to emphasise that the healing isn't just the absence of an affliction, but it is a restoration of a person from the deficiency that caused the sickness.[2] This transformation of the person is alluded to in the rearranging of the letters of צרוע to form עצור, meaning "ceasing to be."[3]

This commitment to the internal work necessary to return—to the ideal, to community, to God—is at the core of repentance and is a powerful form of atonement itself. We find this spotlighted in the tragic story of Elisha Ben Avuyah, later known as Acher. He was one of the four Rabbis who entered into the Orchard, and as a result of his experience, he became an apostate.[4]

A heavenly voice emerged saying: "Return, wayward children[5]—except for Acher/שׁוּבוּ בָּנִים שׁוֹבָבִים חוּץ מֵאַחֵר." His student, the great Rebbe Meir, tried to convince him to return and repent, but Acher was convinced that it wasn't possible. The Jerusalem Talmud[6] tells the story that the great sages of the time were invited to Acher's circumcision. As the festivities were under way, two sages were learning with such intense holiness that fire

---

[1] See Alshich.
[2] Rabbanue Yosef Chaim Drashos.
[3] See Rashi on Shmuel 1 21:8.
[4] Bavli Chagigah 15a.
[5] Jeremiah 3:14.
[6] Chaggia chapter 2.

descended and surrounded them. Acher's father Avuyah enters and questions them on why they are trying to burn down his home. They explain that it is the joyful fire of Torah, as it was given at Mt. Sinai. He is so impressed with the power of learning that he dedicates his baby son to a life of Torah study.

Acher mistakenly thought that since his father's intentions were not purely for the sake of heaven, his Torah study was forever tainted. There is only one teaching said in his name in all of the *mishnayos* and it reflects this attitude:

" אֱלִישָׁע בֶּן אֲבוּיָה אוֹמֵר, הַלּוֹמֵד יֶלֶד לְמָה הוּא דוֹמֶה, לִדְיוֹ כְּתוּבָה עַל נְיָר חָדָשׁ. וְהַלּוֹמֵד זָקֵן לְמָה הוּא דוֹמֶה, לִדְיוֹ כְּתוּבָה עַל נְיָר מָחוּק One who learns as a child, to what can he be compared? To ink written on new paper, [which endures. So, the learning of childhood is not forgotten,] and one who learns in old age, to what can he be compared? To ink written on smudged paper."[7]

Our Rabbis[8] teach that had Acher not been discouraged by the Heavenly rejection, and instead channeled his energy to a place of truthful service motivated by the pure intentions of just doing the right thing, it would have been an atonement and elevated him to a lofty level of spirituality from which God would have derived pleasure. Acher didn't fail the test and then get rejected; the rejection was the test.

---

[7] Avos 4:20.
[8] Igra D'Pirka quoting the Chozeh of Lublin.

We find an allusion to this principle in the generation of Noah. The Torah says "וַתִּשָּׁחֵת הָאָרֶץ לִפְנֵי הָאֱלֹקים" The earth became corrupt before God."[9] The Yismach Yisroel[10] reads the verse homiletically, instructing us to combat corruption by looking at the letters that come before the word "God," which add up to 74,[11] the numerical value of the word "עד""—generally understood as until a point, or boundary. On a deeper level, it is a language of adding and not being limited. For example: "בִּטְחוּ בַיהוָה עֲדֵי־עַד/Trust in the LORD for ever and ever"[12] and "שׁוּבָה יִשְׂרָאֵל עַד יְהוָה אֱלֹהֶיךָ כִּי כָשַׁלְתָּ בַּעֲוֹנֶךָ/Return, O Israel, to the LORD your God, for you have fallen because of your sin."[13]

The generation of Noah felt that they had gone past the point of no return, when really the point is that one can always return. Not everyone was acting so badly, but only Noah found grace from God to be saved from the flood.[14]

When the Heavenly voice declared, "Return children," Acher should have heard it as a reminder that just as a child will remain immutably the offspring of their parent, so too God will always be a parent to us, even when we fall short of God's expectations. "Return children" has a

---

[9] Genesis 6:11.
[10] In the name of the Ari Z"l.

[11] אכדטמ.

[12] Isaiah 26:4.
[13] Hosea 14:2.
[14] Midrash Tanchuma Eikev.

numerical value in Hebrew of 416/ת"י/*tav*, an allusion to the letter "ת/*tav*," which governs over grace.[15]

There is an external grace that is superficial, false, and often leads to juvenile expression.[16] That type of "חן" represents חטאת נעורים/youthful sins.[17] The essential grace comes from the faith we must have that as long as we live, we are able to grow out of bad habits and return to the source of good.

Lepers must believe that they are capable of change and rehabilitation in order to be willing to go through the process that will lead to their reintegration. We, too, must always know that transformation is possible; that we are never so thoroughly outside that we cannot be brought back in.

---

[15] R' Avraham Schor.

[16] Proverbs 31:30.

[17] Psalms 25:7 Seforim Hakidoshim.

Acharei Mos - Graceful Focus

כִּי-בַיּוֹם הַזֶּה יְכַפֵּר עֲלֵיכֶם, לְטַהֵר אֶתְכֶם: מִכֹּל, חַטֹּאתֵיכֶם,
לִפְנֵי יְקֹוָק, תִּטְהָרוּ.

For on this day [God] shall provide atonement for you to
cleanse you; from all of your sins before Hashem shall you
be cleansed.

Leviticus 16:30

Life is filled with distractions.[1] Often, we can even miss
what is directly in front of us. Reish Lakish teaches:[2] "A
person doesn't sin unless a *ruach shtus* (a spirit of spacing
out) enters them""—אין אדם עובר עבירה אא"כ נכנס בו
רוח שטות. The verse specifies that we will be cleansed of
all of our sins before God. Since God is everywhere, all of
the time, aren't all sins before Hashem?

---

[1] Reb Tzadok observes the Hebrew word for noise and evil are
related.
[2] Bavli Sotah 3a.

Rabbi Elazar ben Azarya[3] explains that Yom Kippur, specifically, atones for transgressions between a person and God. However, for transgressions between one person and another, Yom Kippur does not atone until the other person is appeased.

Commandments are often put into a binary: those that are **just** between us and God, and those that affect other people. The Chasam Sofer[4] protests this distinction as a false dichotomy. He argues, "When a person wrongs another, a separation occurs as a result, and that same distance is then placed between the offender and God." We are all created in the image of God, the Chasam Sofer explains, so when we don't care properly for another person, we are automatically moving away from their likeness, God.

Just as every *averia ben adom l'chavaro*, interpersonal transgression, is also an *averia ben adom l'Makom*, a transgression against God, the reverse is also true.[5] Whenever a person is acting inappropriately, it has a broader impact on the world. As the Talmud teaches:[6] " עבר עבירה אחת אוי לו שהכריע את עצמו ואת כל העולם לכף חובה "—a person does one sin, woe to them and the entire world that the scales are tipped."

Rabbi Akiva taught: "How fortunate are you, Israel; before Whom are you purified, and Who purifies you? It is your

---

[3] Bavli Yoma 85b.
[4] Quoted by R' Shalom Shvadron.
[5] The sins act as a chatzitza (ben-between).
[6] Bavli Kiddushin 40b.

Father in Heaven."[7] In support of this he brings the following proof text: "The ritual bath of Israel is God,"[8] and explains: "Just as a *Mikveh* purifies the impure, so too, the Holy One, Blessed be God, purifies Israel." The comparison to a ritual bath is intended to extend the criterion of a total immersion to repentance.[9] Just as the *Mikveh* only purifies when a person first removes anything that would separate themselves from the water, so too a person must cleanse their heart from anything that gets in the way of being close to God.[10]

In the famous prayer of *Avinu Malkeinu*, Our Father Our King, we say "*chatanu lefanecha*/we have sinned before you." It is understood in the mystical tradition[11] as an acknowledgment of the *chesaron*, or lacking,[12] in that we have not been living face to face with God.[13]

The Thirteen Attributes of Mercy, which are the mechanism through which we are forgiven on Yom Kippur, are predicated on God being in front of us:[14] "I will make all My goodness pass **before you**, and I will proclaim **before you** the name LORD, *and I will grant the grace that I will grant and show the compassion that I will show.*" We have to be aware of, and focus on, God's goodness in

---

[7] Bavli Yoma 85b.

[8] Jeremiah 17:13.

[9] Meor HaTorah.

[10] Mikvah is also a language of Tikvah hope. See Divrie Yona.

[11] See Tikunei Zohar 91b.

[12] Kings 1 1:21 see Rashi there.

[13] Ahavas Shalom.

[14] Exodus 33:19.

order to merit this type of grace. The Talmud[15] gives three examples of grace that are achieved by an acute awareness of God's presence. The commentaries[16] connect them to three epic events: the Exodus from Egypt, the giving of the Torah at Mount Sinai, and entering the Land of Israel"—moments of great collective concentration.

The numerical value of grace is 58. Three times 58 is 174, the same value as כסף זהב—silver and gold.[17] We all naturally pursue the things that we believe are valuable, but often don't appreciate the treasure of God's accessibility.

---

[15] Bavli Sota 47a.
[16] See Ben Yehoyada.
[17] Ibid.

Kedoshim - Graceful Love

לֹא-תִקֹּם וְלֹא-תִטֹּר אֶת-בְּנֵי עַמֶּךָ, וְאָהַבְתָּ לְרֵעֲךָ כָּמוֹךָ: אֲנִי, יְהוָה

You shall not take revenge nor shall you bear a grudge against the members of your people; you shall love your fellow as you love yourself – I am Hashem.

Leviticus 19:18

Reb Aron of Karlin taught that if one wants to know how one is doing as a lover of God, one should do an accounting of one's love for God's children; then one will know one's true level of love for God. The only other place in the Torah where the word "ואהבת"—and you shall love—is found is with the commandment to love God. "Love Hashem, your God"[1] has the same numerical value in Hebrew as "Love your neighbor like yourself, I am Hashem."

---

[1] Deuteronomy 6:5.

It is perhaps for this reason that we are given this mitzvah here in Kedoshim. The Imrie Noam notes that the word "Kedoshim" is plural and alludes to these two opportunities to generate holiness through love. Two times the numerical value of קדש (holy) also equals "ואהבת לרעך כמו"/Love your neighbor like yourself. Rashi explains[2] that this *parsha* was read at the gatherings of the entire assembly of Israel, because the majority of the essentials of Torah depend upon it.

This principle of loving another as a way of connecting to "I am Hashem" is articulated by the Ari z"l[3] as follows: "A person must accept upon themselves the commandment to love another as themselves before they pray, for whatever one does for God, they must also do for all of God's children." The book of Leviticus opens with this teaching as well: "When a person (singular) among you offers…you shall bring your offering (plural)."

In the *medrash's*'s exploration of why everyone needed to gather to hear this *parsha*, Rabbi Levi answers, "because the Ten Commandments are incorporated into it." The *medrash* cites a corresponding verse for each of the ten commandments, and the verse that is quoted as representing the commandment of "don't covet" is "loving your neighbor." Nachmanides explains that when we increase our love for one another, and we are happy

---

[2] Leviticus 19:1.
[3] Shar HaKavanas.

when good things happen to others, we lose the ability to be jealous or vengeful.

When God asks us to be holy, at the beginning of the *parsha*, the point of departure is our similarity: "because I am holy." Loving one another as one loves oneself asks one to overcome the perception that we are too different, distinct, or dissimilar to ever see our identities as bound up with each other as one. However, often when we see someone as too similar to us, we can feel threatened, insecure, and in competition for our unique offerings.

The Arvei Nachal quotes a dispute between Plato and Aristotle on the source of love—coming either from the ways in which we are comparable to, or the opposite of, each other. He argues that Platonic love, like the wealthy person pursuing the poor to offer charity,[4] isn't true love. Rather, it's a self-focused love acquired through kindness to another. This works in both directions, as the *medrash* teaches, "More than the person who is wealthy does for the person who is poor, the poor person does for the wealthy."

When two people need each other, like a buyer and a seller, each supports the other and benefits from the relationship. In a dynamic where there isn't a perceived differential of power, the Torah encourages us to put in the effort to love another, particularly when the other is "like ourselves."

---

[4] Bavli Shabbos 104a.

The Aristotelian model, which is less commonly achieved, asks us not to seek out what's in it for us, but to cleave to and elevate the lovablity of the other. This is primarily accomplished when we are first able to see ourselves as lovable, and then, because we see each other as equals, we can engage in truly loving each other.

We find this distinction when Jacob asks Joseph not to bury him in Egypt: "וַיִּקְרָ֣א ׀ לִבְנ֣וֹ לְיוֹסֵ֗ף וַיֹּ֤אמֶר לוֹ֙ אִם־נָ֣א מָצָ֤אתִי חֵן֙ בְּעֵינֶ֔יךָ ...וְעָשִׂ֤יתָ עִמָּדִי֙ חֶ֣סֶד וֶאֱמֶ֔ת—He called to his son, Joseph, if I have found grace in your eyes…please do for me this kindness and truth." Rashi explains that the "kindness that people do for the dead is the kindness of truth, because one doesn't look forward to reciprocation." The Malbim comments that the inclusion of both "son" and "Joseph" alludes to Jacob making his request on two different fronts. As a son, Joseph had certain obligations to honor his father's wishes. But, as a person, he made a different kind of ask, predicated on the recognition of grace.

Rebbi Akiva said about loving another as ourselves, "This is a great principle of the Torah." The Sadigura Rebbe understood "ourselves" as meaning the way that we, ourselves, treat each other. God then reciprocates, and treats us in that same way. Our actions towards each other define our levels of holiness and indicate our true love for God.

Emor - Graceful Progress

וּסְפַרְתֶּם לָכֶם, מִמָּחֳרַת הַשַּׁבָּת, מִיּוֹם הֲבִיאֲכֶם, אֶת-עֹמֶר
הַתְּנוּפָה: שֶׁבַע שַׁבָּתוֹת, תְּמִימֹת תִּהְיֶינָה.

You shall count for yourselves, from the morrow of the
rest of the day, from the day when you bring the omer of
the waving, seven weeks, they shall be complete.

Leviticus 23:15

We find the "Exodus of Egypt" mentioned fifty times in
the Torah,[1] just as the world was created with fifty gates of
wisdom.[2] We also find that when the Israelites left Egypt
they were on the 49th level of spiritual impurity,[3] and on
the brink of reaching spiritual annihilation. Remarkably,
only seven weeks later when they stood at Mount Sinai,
they had reached the 49th level of holiness.[4]

---

[1] Gra.
[2] Bavli Rosh Hashana 21b.
[3] Zohar P' Yisro.
[4] Rokeach.

Every year we re-experience the transition, from going out of Egypt to receiving the Torah, by counting the 49 days of the *omer*. It is intended to be a deeply personal and individualized process of working on one's own evolution and development. The Talmud[5] understands the word "לכם"/you, as "each and every one" shall count for yourself.

These seven weeks are described in the verse as *temimot*, perfect and whole. Rashi explains *temimot* as meaning complete, in that we must begin counting on the second night of Passover, so that the first day of counting isn't deficient. The *medrash* though, understands *temimot* not as a technically complete count, but as complete in a spiritual sense. The *medrash* explains:

אֵימָתַי הֵן תְּמִימוֹת? בִּזְמַן שֶׁיִּשְׂרָאֵל עוֹשִׂין רְצוֹנוֹ שֶׁל מָקוֹם

"When are these [seven weeks] complete? When Israel is doing the will of God."

Clearly, something about the verse is bothering the *medrash* enough that it was moved to reframe it. What does carrying out the Divine will have to do with counting to 49? Additionally, the task of this period of time is specifically to shift the negative into the positive. Rav Vachtfolgel *z"tl* observes that this is why the word "שבתות"/Shabbats are used, as opposed to *shavuot*, meaning weeks—because it is about sanctifying oneself

---

[5] Bavli Menachot 65b.

like the *shabbos*. How, then, are we meant to see the past as perfect if we are invested in changing it for the future?

The Ksav V'kabala explains *temimut* as an indicator of quality, not quantity. When a person is focused on doing their best, whatever that might be, it is called complete. It is so specific to the moment that even the same person should be seen differently, depending on where they are positioned.

Our rabbis also see an allusion in the verse to Abraham, who is told *lech-lecha*, go for yourself. The *medrash* points out that God said those words to Abraham earlier in his spiritual journey, when he first left his father's home, and again many years later, when he was commanded to sacrifice his son Isaac. The *medrash* continues by saying, "and we don't know which was a greater test." An explanation is given, by the Slonimer Rebbe, that both of these tests were equally challenging, because they reflected where Abraham was at the time. Comparing the two doesn't help in evaluating the degree of difficulty at the moment.

We find a similar framing of the *tam*, the "simple son," in the Haggadah. The Vilna Gaon sees him as the counterpoint to the wicked son, since they are each equally focused on either coming closer to, or further away from God. Jacob too is described[6] as a "simple man who sat in

---

[6] Genesis 25:27.

tents." Jacob was simple in that he had no complexity of competing interests besides just doing the right thing.

Perhaps this is what the *medrash* is coming to answer: How can you claim that the seven weeks of the *omer* are *tam*—pure, perfect, and pristine—when it is clearly a work in progress? The important lesson being taught here is that the ideal is in flux. As we do our best to grow and change, every point along the way is *tamim*, or perfect. As we grow, so does the goodness, but those advancements don't minimize or cancel the past.

It is for this reason that we find in Psalms,[7] "Grace and glory does Hashem bestow; God withholds no goodness from those who walk in perfect innocence (בְּתָמִים)." Two people can do or say the same thing, but it can land very differently for each.[8] *Chein*/grace is the difference in the way the action is perceived, and it is determined by the intention and effort of the person acting in the moment.

If we can't appreciate the changes that we are making for the good, because the comparison to the past highlights our shortcomings, we inhibit and deter future development. In repenting for unintentional transgressions, we acknowledge that "had I known then what I know now, I would have acted differently." When we are trying as hard as we can to develop into the best version of ourselves in each moment, we immediately come to learn that the ceiling quickly becomes the floor. In

---

[7] 84:12.
[8] Pele Yoetz.

reflecting back on earlier times "when we just didn't know any better," we need to be critical of society and the factors that contributed to that environment. But knowing better, and acting differently because of that wisdom today, is a holy accomplishment.

Behar - Graceful Fluidity

אֶת-שַׁבְּתֹתַי תִּשְׁמֹרוּ, וּמִקְדָּשִׁי תִּירָאוּ׃ אֲנִי, יְהוָה.

My Sabbaths shall you observe and My Sanctuary shall you revere – I am Hashem.

Leviticus 26:2

Shabbat is an invitation for a time of deep and personal intimacy with God. It is also a time of great expansiveness to support the multifaceted spectrums of connectivity. We are told that on Shabbat we are given an additional soul to accommodate the soul's dominance over the body, particularly in an arc of gender sensitivities.[1]

Although there is a dispute about which day of the month the Torah was given, "According to everyone it was given on the *shabbos*."[2] Shavuot is seen as the wedding between the Jewish people and God, which we prepare for by

---

[1] See Shabbos as an All Gender Experience.
[2] Bavli Shabbat 86b.

counting seven weeks from the blood of Passover.[3] The two tablets were given to affect the *kiddushin* under the *chuppah* of Mount Sinai.[4] Tradition also teaches that this is re-experienced every week with *shabbos*.[5] The Ari *z"l* says that it is reflected in the unique blessing in the Friday night prayer "*Atah Kedashta*"—which can either mean "you sanctified," or "you betrothed."

God's identity in this relationship, like the People of Israel's, is gender fluid. We find the Jewish people as a bride, אֲרוּסָתוֹ שֶׁל הַקָּבָּ"ה יִשְׂרָאֵל—God's bride is Israel,[6] and the tablets are the *shtar*—marriage document[7]—to the bride. Even the standard structure of the wedding blessing today, "Who sanctified your people Israel through *chuppah* and *kiddushin*," is referring to the wedding between us and God at Sinai.[8]

We also find that the Jewish people are referred to as the groom, marrying the Torah,[9] where God is the father of the bride,[10] and the *mikdash*—sanctuaries that we are commanded to build—are quarters for God, as God is our in-law who just wants to be close to us, wherever we are.

---

[3] Zohar.
[4] Haflah.
[5] Igeres Hatyul.
[6] Rashi, Exodus 34:1.
[7] Baal Haturim, Exodus 19:4.
[8] Sheta Mekubetzes.
[9] Bavli Pesachim 49b.
[10] Shemot Rabbah 33:1.

Unfortunately, the honeymoon is short lived. Just forty days later, we sinned against God in an adulterous act with the golden calf.[11] God's identity as the Creator necessitates our exclusivity in faithful monotheism. It also translates into the validation of this identity through the celebration of *shabbos*. The Rabbis go so far as to equate observing *shabbos* with fulfillment of the entire Torah.[12]

Maimonides, in concluding his laws of forbidden relationships, writes that "the greatest antidote to acting inappropriately is to turn oneself and one's thoughts to words of Torah and immerse their mind in wisdom, because inappropriate thoughts do not rule in one's mind except in the mind of one whose heart is turned away from wisdom. Regarding wisdom it is said, 'It is a beloved hind, arousing grace. . . You shall be obsessed with her love.'"[13]

The Talmud[14] explains the comparison, teaching that "matters of Torah are cherished by those who study them each and every hour like the first hour." Each part of this verse, according to the Vilna Gaon, refers to one of the four layers of the Torah's פרדס/*pardes*, and their corresponding levels of physical and intellectual intimacy.

One of the consequences of the breaking of the first set of tablets, at the sin of the Golden Calf, is the necessity for the oral law.[15] The Torah is referred to as both male and

---

[11] Rashi, Exodus 32:20 and Bavli Avodah Zarah 44a.
[12] Ohr Hachaim 26:2.
[13] Proverbs 5:19.
[14] Bavli Eruvin 52b.
[15] Shar Yissaschar.

female, even in the same verse.[16] It is also understood that
the written Torah skews masculine, while the oral Torah
leans towards the feminine.[17] Reb Zadok[18] teaches that,
although the entire Torah is from God, the written
represents God's wisdom while the oral is from Israel's.
The Zohar's[19] famous teaching that God, Torah, and Israel
are one can be understood as the process of God and the
Jewish people sanctifying their union at Sinai through the
written Torah, and then coming together with the oral
law.[20]

There is no grace like the fulfillment of the Torah— אין חן
כקיום התורה.[21] However, unlike *shabbos*, which comes
every seven days with or without us, we are responsible for
showing up to do our part in furthering the acceptance,
understanding, and production of Torah. The more we
revisit it, the newer, deeper, and more personal it becomes.
As we prepare for Shavuot, let us feel empowered and
embodied to expand our connectivity to the holiday
beyond just our lived experience, by experiencing it as part
of the collective whole.

[16] Exodus 12:49.
[17] Bavli Kiddushin 2b Ben Yehoyada.
[18] Dover Tzedek.
[19] 3:73a.
[20] R' Eliyahu Baruch.
[21] Shevet Mussar.

Bechukotai - Graceful Investment

אִם-בְּחֻקֹּתַי, תֵּלֵכוּ; וְאֶת-מִצְוֹתַי תִּשְׁמְרוּ, וַעֲשִׂיתֶם אֹתָם.

If you will walk in the way of My statutes and observe My commandments and perform them.

Leviticus 26:3

One of the many consequences of the original sin is that we must now labor to understand the Torah.[1] The intimacy that God shared with us in the Garden of Eden included open access to God's wisdom, but after we sinned we must struggle to gain understanding. Rashi[2] explains "If you will walk in the way of My statutes" as "שֶׁתִּהְיוּ עֲמֵלִים בַּתּוֹרָה/you should toil in Torah."[3] In our world, after the sin, God and God's intentions are hidden. This "world"/עלם/*olam* is also the word for "hidden", and

---

[1] Toras HaRemez.
[2] Quoting the Sifra.
[3] Bal Hatutim observes these two phrases have the same numerical value as well.

an anagram for "toil"/עמל/*amal,* alluding to our ability to return to that intimacy and knowledge through the effort of learning Torah.

God instructs us to continually improve by walking in the way of God's statutes. Indeed, Rabbi Yonason Eibeschitz claims that it is the human capacity for progress that differentiates us from angels. Angels are static in their roles, whereas we are commanded to "תלכו/go."[4] Yet, somewhat ironically, we are told to go in the ways of God's חוקים/*chukim,* even though חוקים are defined as laws whose purpose cannot be understood.

The Talmud,[5] perhaps bothered by this question, recontextualizes the verse by stating:

אין אם אלא
לשון תחנונים

[The word] "if"
is exclusively a
language of
supplication.

God desires that we labor in the study of Torah.[6] One way to understand this is that part of God's perfection is the need to give goodness, and therefore God wants us to access goodness through the holy process of learning.[7] But

[4] See Tam V'das for an alternative approach.
[5] Bavli Avodah Zarah 5a.
[6] Toras Kohanim.
[7] R' Shmuel Rozofsky.

what good is studying something that we can't really understand? More specifically, the language of desire implies a yearning for something that is currently lacking.[8] How are we meant to understand our contribution to God's Torah through the study of that which we can't truly grasp?

King Solomon's timeless pedagogical advice[9] of: " חֲנֹךְ לַנַּעַר עַל־פִּי דַרְכּוֹ, educate a child according to their way" is recognized by the Zera Kodesh as an arc of spiritual ascension. At the start, a student needs personalized instruction and a clear sense of comprehension to be motivated to continue their studies. After maturing, though, they can reach a higher level of drive—not for explanations but for opportunities to connect.

This effort, as opposed to an intellectual approach, provides a worthiness that is rewarded beyond the limited vessel of our cerebral capabilities. אם־בחקתי תלכו ואת— the first letter of each of the first four words of the verse can be arranged to form the word אבות/ancestors, which alludes to the merit of the Thirteen Attributes of Mercy that our ancestors received and from which we still benefit.[10] The Patriarchs collectively lived 510/שיר years,[11] and this is reflected in the first word of the Torah, בראשית, which can be rearranged to form שיר אבת (the song of our ancestors). The Zera Kodesh continues to explain that

---

[8] Karbon Aharon.
[9] Proverbs 22:6.
[10] Zera Kodesh.
[11] Semos Rabbah 1:1.

the first of the Thirteen Attributes of Mercy, א-ל, which has a numerical value of 31, when multiplied by 13 equals 403, the value of אבת, ancestors.

The Zohar[12] teaches that Torah, God, and the Jewish people are all simultaneously hidden and revealed. He explains that the secrets of the Torah, and the reasons behind its statutes, are deeper than our ability to intuit or naturally comprehend. However, they are revealed to people who elevate themselves, paralleling the gift of grace that we can't obtain on our own, but that is granted when we put in the effort. This is how the Talmud[13] understand the verse[14] "And I will be gracious to whom I will be gracious": אַף עַל פִּי שֶׁאֵינוֹ הָגוּן, even to those who are not fitting [of self acquisition]".

The goal of spiritual practice is to train ourselves to go in God's ways. As King David said in Psalm 119, "I have considered my ways, and have turned my feet to Your decrees."[15] The *medrash*[16] explains that because King David considered his ways through spiritual reflection, he began to feel a natural alignment and pull to "walk in the ways" of study and prayer. Things that are difficult when we first start, often become easier as we become accustomed to them. When we put in the effort and truly go all in, we are supported beyond our means. As the Talmud[17] testifies:

---

[12] 3:73a.
[13] Bavli Berachot 7a.
[14] Exodus 33:19.
[15] Psalms 119:59.
[16] Vayikrah Rabbah 35:1.
[17] Bavli Makos 10b.

בדרך שאדם רוצה לילך בה מוליכין אותו, along the path a person wishes to proceed on, they are taken.

Sefer Bamidbar

Bamidbar - Graceful Flag

אִישׁ עַל-דִּגְלוֹ בְאֹתֹת לְבֵית אֲבֹתָם, יַחֲנוּ בְּנֵי יִשְׂרָאֵל: מִנֶּגֶד,
סָבִיב לְאֹהֶל-מוֹעֵד יַחֲנוּ.

The Children of Israel shall encamp, each man at his
banner according to the signs of their father's house, at a
distance surrounding the Tent of Meeting shall they
encamp.

Bamidbar 2:2

Our collective pursuit of unity requires the expansion of
our individual identities, not an erasure of them. The 49
days of counting the *omer* correspond to the 49 different
ways that Moshe expounded on the Torah, and encourage
us to harvest the good that exists in the paths of others as
a way of advancing our own development. The *medrash*[1]
finds support for this from the verse,[2] "[God] brought me

---

[1] Bamidbar Rabbah 2:3.
[2] Song of Songs 2:4.

to the banquet room and [God's] banner of love was over
me—וְדִגְלוֹ‎. Banner/וְדִגְלוֹ‎. "הֱבִיאַ֙נִי֙ אֶל־בֵּ֣ית הַיָּ֔יִן וְדִגְל֥וֹ עָלַ֖י אַהֲבָֽה׃‎
has a numerical value of 49, an allusion to the various
pairings of attributes–מדה‎ (also numerically 49)–with each
other.

We are taught[3] that all of God's attributes are applied
measure for measure–*midah k'neged midah,* שכל מדותיו של
הקב"ה מדה כנגד מדה‎. The Code of Jewish Law[4] instructs
us to always read this Torah portion before Shavuot, and it
is seen as part of our preparation for the annual re-
experiencing of Mt. Sinai. The Munkatcher Rebbe points
out that the word "*neged*" is a reference to the giving of the
Torah,[5] where Israel was "opposite the mountain." *Neged* is
a contranym, a word that has contradicting meanings, and
here means both corresponding to and in opposition.

We first find this word in the Torah when God forms a
"helpmate"–*ezer k'negdo*–for Adam.[6] The Talmud[7] sees this
strange phrase as conditional: if one is worthy, then they
will have a partner; if not–an opponent.

Rashi also deploys the word "*k'neged*" to describe the
arrangement of the different tribes that Bilam observes
when he comes to curse the people of Israel.[8] However,
when Bilam saw that "the openings of the tents were not

---

[3] Bavli Sanhedrin 90a.
[4] 428:4.
[5] Exodus 19:2.
[6] Genesis 2:18.
[7] Bavli Yevamos 63a.
[8] Numbers 24:2.

aligned/*k'neged* to each other" (and therefore there was privacy between them) he offered the blessing of *Ma Tovu*: "How goodly are your tents."

R' Asher Rapshitz[9] explains that each one of us has a unique "opening" to spiritual practice. He understands the obligation to ask ourselves, "When will my actions reach those of my ancestors Abraham, Isaac, and Jacob?"[10] not to mean that we should try to imitate our ancestors and simply act as they did, but that just as our forefathers were each unique and brought new attributes to Divine service, like kindness and strength, so too should we bring a new blend of ourselves to spiritual practice.

This is also alluded to in the Talmudic principle[11] of תַּעֲשֶׂה וְלֹא מִן הֶעָשׂוּי–We should prepare [the sukkah], and not just use that which has already been prepared.[12] A posture of creative production is not unique to building a sukkah, rather it generates the holiness of our spiritual contributions. They are offerings of our unique makeup.

Exploring who we are and how we are meant to be in the moment is the core of being human. Asking oneself, "What is the right thing for me to do now?" is essential in creating the best outcome, particularly for a pleasant coexistence. The word for encampment–*machene*–is composed of the words מה חן/*ma chein*, "what" and "grace." Understanding what makes us different allows us

---

[9] Ohr Yeshie.
[10] Tana D'bei Eleyahu.
[11] Bavli Succah 11b.
[12] Rav Tov.

to relate appropriately and come closer to each other as our distinct selves.

The way God spoke to Moshe at the burning bush was different from the way God spoke to all of Israel at the giving of the Torah. The Sifra,[13] in comparing and contrasting the two forms of language, says that we can learn from the hermeneutical exegesis known as a *binyan av*. These 13 *midos*, or principles, correspond to the 13 *Midos HaRachamim*, or Attributes of Mercy. According to Reb Lev Yitchak of Berditchev,[14] the *binyan av* corresponds to *chein*/grace. When we can learn from each other and incorporate that knowledge into building better relationships, we develop more gracefulness.

Each one of us has our own flag and special purpose in this world. Sometimes it is to be in support of those around us, and other times it is to be in opposition. The important lesson is to be thoughtful and deliberate in harnessing what is unique about us to improve the world for everyone.

---

[13] Parashat Vayikra.
[14] Kidushas Levi, Exodus, Ki Sisa.

Nasso - Graceful Sons[1]

יָאֵר יְהוָה פָּנָיו אֵלֶיךָ, וִיחֻנֶּךָּ.

May Hashem illuminate [God's] countenance towards you
and endow you with grace.

Bamidbar 6:25

The phrase "toxic masculinity" is in the news and culture a
great deal these days, and is often misunderstood. Rather
than indicate that masculinity is inherently toxic or
harmful, the phrase "toxic masculinity" points to an overly
narrow and repressive definition of manhood, by which
boys and men are taught that the only way to be "a real
man" is through violence, sex, status, and aggression.
Toxic masculinity can be implicated in everything from
school shootings, to sexual harassment, and to
mansplaining. But what does healthy masculinity look like?
What can we learn from the Torah about a more expansive

---

[1] First published with Rabbi Rachel Timoner as "Graceful
Masculinity" for HBI on June 13, 2019.

146

and robust definition of manhood, and about how to heal the toxic forms of masculinity?

In this week's *parsha* we are taught about the *sotah*: a woman whose jealous husband suspects her of being unfaithful. It is clear from the design of the ritual that the *sotah* must undergo, that the problem being addressed is not an actual question of infidelity by the woman, but dangerous possessiveness and entitlement by the man. Here we see the Torah acknowledge the very real and universal emotion of jealousy, understanding that in a society in which a man's honor and status is dependent upon being able to control his wife, such jealousy could be dangerous, even deadly.

The Torah provides a remedy for the man's excessive bitterness and entitlement: the woman is brought before the high priest and must drink a mixture of bitter water and humble earth with God's name dissolved into the mixture. God is willing to have God's holy name erased in order to protect the life and safety of a woman, to heal the wounded heart and pride of a man, and to make room for peace.

The *parsha* immediately proceeds to teach us about the *nazir*, a man who temporarily steps back from society and adopts an ascetic posture of separation. The Talmud explains the juxtaposition of the *sotah* and the *nazir* as Divine advice for men who witness the disgrace of a *sotah*. In order to break the cycle of excessive possessiveness and entitlement, a male witness to the *sotah* ritual should accept upon himself a period of excessive self-denial and restraint.

It is as if he must swing from one extreme to another as a corrective, in order to eventually find a middle path.

It is noteworthy that this chapter ends with that middle path, a three-part paternal blessing and message for Aaron and his sons. This is also the blessing that is traditionally offered from parents to their children every Shabbat. The three verse blessing starts with a request for protection/guardianship and concludes with an ask for peace. What sticks out is the middle verse, which reads: "May Hashem illuminate God's countenance toward you and endow you with grace/חן."

We find an interesting connection between grace and masculinity in early mystical sources. Sefer Yetzirah, the Book of Creation, says that God made the letter "ת"/"*tav*" king over grace, and that the letter corresponds to the day of Shabbat. It has been observed that when you insert the "*tav*" in the middle of "grace," you form the word "*chasson*/חתן," the Hebrew term for groom.

Our rabbis teach that the essence of grace comes from Shabbat. After man's sin of crossing a boundary in the Garden of Eden (where despite being able to eat from all of the other trees, being told "no" to just one thing was too much), Shabbat was a time to pause in an atmosphere of God's total acceptance and love, an atmosphere that enabled him to reflect and change. R' Tzodok writes that the blessing of "And God blessed the seventh day,"[2] was the blessing of חן/grace.

The gift of Shabbat is the gift of God's grace. We experience acceptance of, and gratitude for, the world as it is; without the need to control, possess, or dominate and with which we feel loved and "good enough" just as we are. The Talmud teaches us that we are meant to learn from the way in which God models for us the proper way to act. God's behavior stands in contrast to the jealous husband in the ritual of the *sotah*. Although God created us, God does not act as if God owns us. In fact, God values above all our free will and ability to make choices. A groom, if behaving like God, will deeply honor the free will of his spouse and aspire to be worthy of such a partner. Filled with חן/grace, he will feel accepted and loved for who he is, and ready to accept and love his partner.

God, the source of all genders, has many gendered attributes and is also the source of all good. The humility and respect that God has for the space that we take up in this world, despite the actual power differential that exists between the Creator and Their creations, provides an important template for our interpersonal interactions, where the power differences are only a social construction. May we all find the illumination necessary to create a society where all gender expressions are reflections of the Divine, and all are filled with grace.

---

[2] Genesis 2:3.

Beha'alotcha - Graceful Lightness

וַיֹּאמֶר מֹשֶׁה אֶל-יְהוָה, לָמָה הֲרֵעֹתָ לְעַבְדֶּךָ, וְלָמָּה לֹא-מָצָתִי חֵן,
בְּעֵינֶיךָ: לָשׂוּם, אֶת-מַשָּׂא כָּל-הָעָם הַזֶּה--עָלָי.

Moses said to Hashem: "Why have you done evil to your
servant, why haven't I found favor in your eyes, that you
place the burden of the entire people upon me?"

Numbers 11:11

When we sense God's closeness, our struggles feel holy,
not heavy. As the clarity of our purpose increases, internal
resistance decreases–until the only opposition is coming
from outside of us. When Adam and Eve were first
created, there was no doubt about who they were in
relation to God. Then, the snake came along and deceived
them. By ingesting the forbidden fruit, Adam and Eve
internalized the evil inclination, and then needed to battle
within themselves, to purge that voice of distraction that
tries to divert our power away from goodness.

As God spoke this world into existence, through different
utterances, the verses confirm, "and it was so"/"כן,"

except for the creation of light, where the word "כן" is
missing. The rabbis explain that God was concerned that
the light would be misused, and so although God said,
"Let there be light," God concealed and separated it for
the righteous in the future.[1] This primordial light finds
expression when Aharon lights the menorah and it is
marked with the word "כן."[2]

In the Genesis narrative, the word "light"/אור/ohr is
mentioned five times in the process of light's formation.
As a reference to that hidden light, we also find the word
"*ohr*" five times in this week's Torah portion. The light of
the menorah also represents the light of the Torah and its
wisdom, as the Talmud says: "the one who wants to be
wise should face south,"[3] for that is where the menorah
was placed.[4]

This wisdom, a consequence of the original light, is alluded
to in the letter *aleph*,[5] as the verse says:[6] וַאֲאַלֶּפְךָ כְמָה. The
letter *aleph*/"א" is formed with a pair of a two *yuds* and two
vavs—וי—one on top and one on the bottom[7] having a
numerical value of 32 and corresponding to the 32 paths
of wisdom and the heart/*lev*/לב, the source of this
understanding.

---

[1] Bavli Chagigah 12a.
[2] Emunas Eticha.
[3] Bavli Bava Basra 25b.
[4] Maharsha.
[5] HaTzvi V'Hatzadik.
[6] Job 33:33.
[7] Megaleh Amukos 164.

Moses had a light that shone from his face, and according to Tikunei Zohar,[8] it originated in the light of the Garden of Eden. Moses achieved this by correcting the sin of Adam and replacing the *ohr*/skin/עור with *ohr*/light/אור, restoring the prelapsarian partnership with God.

The Israelites had also acquired an elevated level, above the natural physical order, and were sustained by the *mana*. However, when they asked for meat, they no longer wanted to subside in such a spiritual plane and desired more physicality. They lowered themselves and created a separation from God, just as Adam and Eve did in the garden, desiring the desire for choice.

It is in this moment that Moses, as their teacher, felt the absence of this light and the subsequent weight of carrying the people without the same Divine assistance.[9] The word for "found" in the phrase "Why haven't I found favor in your eyes –וְלָמָּה לֹא-מָצָתִי חֵן בְּעֵינֶיךָ" is missing the aleph.[10] It was the people's desire for meat that once again forced the exchange of the light for skin, and is alluded to in the word following "grace" "eynecha" literally "your eyes" but also meaning "your letter ע."[11]

Having grace makes it easier for others to become close to us, and for us to be close to others. Knowing with certainty that God expects us to take care of one another,

---

[8] Genesis 36b.
[9] R' Vulli.
[10] Iben Ezra.
[11] Yeytev Lev.

makes the desire for anything else no longer an option to choose from. While the work is still challenging, it is not burdensome. Feeling this partnership with God reminds us that with God's help, nothing is impossible.

Shelach - Graceful Takings

שְׁלַח-לְךָ אֲנָשִׁים, וְיָתֻרוּ אֶת-אֶרֶץ כְּנַעַן, אֲשֶׁר-אֲנִי נֹתֵן, לִבְנֵי
יִשְׂרָאֵל: אִישׁ אֶחָד אִישׁ אֶחָד לְמַטֵּה אֲבֹתָיו, תִּשְׁלָחוּ–כֹּל, נָשִׂיא
בָהֶם

Send forth for yourself men and let them spy out the Land
of Canaan that I give to the Children of Israel; one man
each from his fathers' tribe shall you send, every one a
leader among them.

Numbers 13:2

Before Moses sent the scouts to report back on the land of
Israel there was a sensitivity training of sorts, on the
proper way to speak. Rashi observes that the spies are sent
right after the incident of Miriam, who was punished for
the way she spoke against her brother. Rashi notes, "these
wicked ones saw [what happened to her] and yet didn't
learn from it." The phrase that Rashi uses to describe their
failure is the lack of "taking mussar-מוּסָר וְלֹא לָקְחוּ", often
translated as rebuke, and speaks to one's capacity to
become more aware of a better way of being and to then
to grow into that better person.

154

Our ability to break cycles and patterns of negativity is generally contingent upon our optimism and hopefulness in achieving a different outcome. If we can't see the positive potential that exists, it is much harder to try and actualize it. Lashon hara, speaking badly about another, at its core is highlighting the worst, and not the potential for improvement.

The Talmud[1] offers the incident of the spies as the prooftext for the severity of lashon hara. "If one who defames the wood and rocks [of Israel] received such [a severe punishment], then one who defames another person, all the more so." From the Talmud's perspective, it seems that we are meant to learn from speaking badly about the land, that doesn't have feelings or a soul, to know not to treat people that way. However Rashi, quoting the Medrish, blames the spies for not learning from speaking badly about a person to apply it to the land. The punishment of wandering in the desert for forty years seems quite excessive for not being about to intuit this a fortiori!

Nachmanides implies that the essence of the sin of the spies was a lack of faith in God providing safe passage. Rashi explains that before this sin, they could have gone in peacefully without weapons and settled the land, but because of their lack of faith, they would eventually need to engage in the natural way of fighting for the land.

---

[1] Bavli Arachin 15a.

Indeed the word "שלח" "sh'lach" is an anagram of "חלש" meaning weak. They only needed to scout out the land because their faith in God's ability to guide and protect them was deficient. They couldn't imagine a different version that prioritized the spiritual over the physical.

When they spoke out about the land, they could have focused on the positive, but chose not to. This is no different from the root of Miriam's claim to Moses, assuming that he was like other prophets and therefore should have remained married.

Rabbi E. B. Finkel points out that Rashi understands the problem with the spies not as a technical issue of speaking badly, but for not learning the lesson and working on themselves. A person who speaks lashon hara is negatively affected when they diminish the Divine image in another person, and even the holiness of an object. He quotes R' Chaim Shmuelevitz that the punishment of 40 years is not for the one moment of speaking badly, but for the entire 40 days where they were carrying these negative views.

Perhaps this is why Rashi uses the language of "taking mussar". It is not enough to learn or study in a proscriptive way, but a person needs to proactively deliberate and take the lessons, even if no one is giving them, to best know how to act. The Medresh,[2] teaching about the value of חן, explains that the source of good, in grace, is in taking a truth and applying it to new situations.

---

[2] Mishlei 22:1.

We find similar advice in the Sefas Emes[3] who encourages us to guard and protect against anything that comes to minimize the Divine Image in humanity, because it is that image that produces grace. God's expectations of us extend beyond our actions, to the root of our desire to learn from the world around us. Being able to appreciate the holiness of the land requires us to first be sensitive to the even greater holiness of people, and the potential for a peaceful coexistence.

---

[3] Parshas Noach.

Korach - Graceful Reward

וַיַּקְהֵל עֲלֵיהֶם קֹרַח אֶת-כָּל-הָעֵדָה, אֶל-פֶּתַח אֹהֶל מוֹעֵד; וַיֵּרָא
כְבוֹד-יְהוָה, אֶל-כָּל-הָעֵדָה

Korach gathered the entire assembly against them at the entrance of the Tent of Meeting, and the glory of God appeared to the entire assembly.

Numbers 16:19

Our freedom to make choices is what holds us responsible for them. The Talmud[1] teaches: "on the path that a person wants to go, they lead the person". The Chidushei Aggados explains the odd use of the plural "they" as the angelic forces that combine with our thoughts, speech, and actions to manifest our desires in the physical world.

However, because of God's kindness, while permission is given to choose poorly, support is offered to us when we want to go in the right direction. A proof text, offered by

---

[1] Bavli Makos 10b.

the Talmud for the above teaching, is from Proverbs:[2] "אִם־לַלֵּצִים הוּא־יָלִיץ וְלַעֲנָוִים יִתֶּן־חֵן" - If [one is attracted] to the scoffers, they will scoff; but [if one is attracted] to the humble, they will find grace".

One of the students of the Gra[3] points out the structural asymmetry of the verse; why doesn't it simply end with a parallel to the beginning of "they will be humble"? He observes the word "יליץ", to scoff, is the same letters as "יציל", to save, which is coming to teach us that if a person chooses to go down the wrong path, they are allowed and will not be saved from that decision. However, when it comes to a person's intention to do good, God not only sanctions it, but also provides even more goodness through the gift of God's grace. This is alluded to in the numerical value of God's name spelled out, and grace, both being 58: חן = יו"ד ה"י וא"ו ה"ה.

Psalms[4] begins: אַשְׁרֵי הָאִישׁ אֲשֶׁר ׀ לֹא הָלַךְ בַּעֲצַת רְשָׁעִים וּבְמוֹשַׁב לֵצִים לֹא יָשָׁב ... - Happy is the person who doesn't go in the counsel of the wicked...and who isn't sitting in the company of mockers. The Medrash[5] explains that the end of this verse is referring to Korach.

---

[2] 3:34.

[3] רמד"ו.

[4] 1:1.
[5] Tehillim 1:13.

Additionally, Rashi attributes Korach's ability to gather people in opposition to Moshe through words of ליצנות - mockery.

It is hard to imagine how Korach was able to rally so many impressive people against Moshe, after they had all witnessed his role in the Exodus of Egypt and the receiving of the Torah. What power does this type of speech have to seduce people away from the miraculous events, and God's goodness, that they had all just experienced?

The Imrei Chaim answers that experiences or insights that don't enter a person's heart, simply will not make an impression. Without this impact, there is no change, and the person remains the same. Rashi[6] understands that it is humility that permits a person's heart to be open to the experience and to be affected by it.

It is perhaps for this reason that the verse in Proverbs positions humility as the opposite of mockery. Scoffing at something deflects it, and the impact of it's truth, away from a person. If one isn't willing to take something important seriously, one cannot appreciate its value.

This negative character trait is also the source of *machlokes* - infighting. There are many things that reasonable people can disagree about. However, if there isn't a real desire to understand another's position, as a tool to better grasp the

---

[6] On Bavli Berachot 7a.

issue, then the default is just to obviate the discussion through ridiculing the other.[7]

According to the Medresh, Korach's children were able to be saved from this fighting because they fulfilled the second verse in Psalms: כִּי אִם בְּתוֹרַת יְהֹוָה חֶפְצוֹ וּבְתוֹרָתוֹ יֶהְגֶּה יוֹמָם וָלָיְלָה - Rather their desire is in the Torah of God, and in one's Torah they toil day and night". When we choose to be discerning and thoughtful, we are able to come together with others doing the same. Even if in the end we don't arrive at the same conclusion, we still benefit from being on the same side of the fight for truth, justice, and peaceful coexistence.

---

[7] Ben Yehoyada Avodah Zarah 55a רצונו לומר האדם הוא שיליץ
אבל לענונים שרואין עצמם אַיָן כמו הצל שהוא עובר ואין הנה הצל
מלוי שלו 'חֵן' 58 שהוא גם כן כמנין דדים 58 אשר בתוך אותיות
'לֵץ' ורק כאן נהפך המספר של 'דדים' למספר 'חן' שהוא מספר כָּבוֹד
הֵן' 58 שזה מורה שמסייעין אותו בהארות אלו שמאירין בו.

Chukkas - Graceful Acceptance

זֹאת חֻקַּת הַתּוֹרָה, אֲשֶׁר-צִוָּה יְהוָה לֵאמֹר: דַּבֵּר אֶל-בְּנֵי
יִשְׂרָאֵל, וְיִקְחוּ אֵלֶיךָ פָרָה אֲדֻמָּה תְּמִימָה אֲשֶׁר אֵין-בָּהּ מוּם,
אֲשֶׁר לֹא-עָלָה עָלֶיהָ, עֹל

This is the statute of the Torah, which Hashem has
commanded saying: Speak to the Children of Israel and
they shall take to you a perfectly red cow, which has no
blemish, which hasn't had a yoke on it.

Numbers 19:2

An interesting, if counterintuitive, aspect of the laws of the
red heifer is that while the ritual of sprinkling its ashes
purifies one who is impure, the pure person performing
the ritual becomes impure. The Talmud[1] asserts that even
King Solomon, the wisest of all people, was baffled by this
law. The verse "All this I tested with wisdom, I thought I
could fathom it [through wisdom], but it eludes me – כָּל-
is "זֹה נִסִּיתִי בַחָכְמָה אָמַרְתִּי אֶחְכָּמָה וְהִיא רְחוֹקָה מִמֶּנִּי

---

[1] Bavli Nidda 9a.

understood by the Tamud as King's Solomon's acknowledgement that wisdom alone could not assist him to comprehend these precepts.

We often have a hard time understanding identities or experiences that are not our own. The rabbis observe this lack of first person engagement as an inhibitor to completely grasping Torah concepts. A person doesn't understand words of Torah until they have stumbled [in them] – אין אדם עומד על דברי תורה אלא אם כן נכשל.[2]

The Ohev Yisrael explains that we naturally think of ourselves as having a proper perspective on things and therefore assume we are going on the right path. However, when life happens and we fall down, we have an opportunity to acknowledge our mistakes in light of the revealed truth of the matter, and to reorient accordingly. This is particularly true of folks who see themselves as "having no blemish".

This, says the Chozeh Lublin, can only happen when a person "hasn't had a yoke [of Torah] on them". In other words, only a person who is unaware of the work that needs to be done in the world, and their role in it, can think that they have attained perfection.

Simply learning about a concept or idea doesn't necessarily deliver the impact or proximity as a heart connection to those affected by the teaching. This is alluded to in the

---

[2] Bavli Gittin 43a.

verse[3] "There is an abundant peace to the lovers of your Torah, and they don't have a stumbling block – שָׁלוֹם רָב לְאֹהֲבֵי תוֹרָתֶךָ וְאֵין־לָמוֹ מִכְשׁוֹל." There is a particular grace and care that is achieved through the love that one has for another as a result of the investment of deep listening and learning.

In Hebrew, the word for ear is ozen / אֹזֶן which has the same numerical value as grace, chein / חֵן.[4] Listening is essential in learning the oral law, and by toiling in it we can broaden and develop our sensitivities to society. The role of grace in this is alluded to in the number of chapters of Mishnayos, 524, equaling the full spelling of the two letters in grace -חֵן-chein: חי"ת נו"ן. Additionally, תלמוד בבלי – Babylonian Talmud also has the numerical value of 524. Through a deep engagement with the oral law, we train ourselves to listen carefully and internalize teachings, even when we do not completely understand them.

We always read and study this portion in preparation for the saddest time of the year, the three weeks leading up to the destruction of the Temple. Our rabbis teach that the Temple was destroyed, and we remain in exile, because of *sinas chinam* – meaning hating people without reason. One of the lessons from studying a law that we can't understand, but nevertheless accept, is that it models how to do the same with people.

---

[3] Psalms 119:165.
[4] AriZ"l.

We don't need to understand another person in order to accept them. One shouldn't have to get to know someone, and then find something positive in them to justify caring about them. We don't need reasons to love people. God's love for us isn't dependent on anything. The unconditional love that God has for us as children should motivate us to extend that *ahavas chinam* – free love – to all of our siblings.

That which is seen as perfect, perhaps conveys impurity to remind us that our path towards perfection necessitates struggle, and that struggle is itself purifying.

Balak - Graceful Protest

וַיִּשָּׂא מְשָׁלוֹ וַיֹּאמַר נְאֻם בִּלְעָם בְּנוֹ בְעֹר וּנְאֻם הַגֶּבֶר שְׁתֻם הָעָיִן׃

He declared his parable and said: "The words of Bilaam son of Beor, the words of the man who is *shetum ha-ayin*."

Numbers 24:3

Bilaam, the famous Midianite prophet, is described as *shetum ha-ayin*, understood by some commentaries as sharp-sighted, and by others as half-blind. Indeed, what Bilaam sees and does not see is critical to his appraisal of the people of Israel.

At first, never having laid eyes on Israel, he agrees to try and curse them. Later, having caught a glimpse of Israel, he is moved to bless them. Then gazing on them fully, he blesses them so powerfully that his words become the start of our daily prayers – *mah tovu ohalecha* Yaakov, how goodly are your tents, Jacob.

This trajectory is what we always hope for – that when we know each other better, we will be less prejudiced and more loving. The Torah is filled with examples of how it is easier to hate from afar. Joseph's brothers see him from a distance and it is then that they plot to get rid of him. Esav wants to kill Jacob when he is not with him, but then when he actually confronts him he embraces and kisses him.

Yet Bilaam is not understood by our tradition as an example of successful bridge-building. His prophecies, though gorgeous, are understood to lead to Israel's subsequent sin at Shittim. As the *midrash*[1] explains:

"One who protests/reproves a person will afterward find more grace than one who speaks with a smooth tongue."[2]

"One who protests/reproves" – this is Moses . . .

"Find more grace" – as it is said, You have found grace in My eyes.[3]

"Than one who speaks with a smooth tongue" – this is Bilaam who flattered Israel with his prophecies and their hearts filled with hubris and they sinned in Shittim.

Although Bilaam sees Israel and speaks beautifully about them, the Midrash complains that he does not authentically engage with them. His words are seen as superficial flattery that inflates Israel's sense of self and leads them to a gruesome fall. By contrast, Moses has a

---

[1] Devarim Rabbah 1:2.
[2] Proverbs 28:23.
[3] Exodus 33:12.

trustworthy relationship with Israel, filled with love, expectations, and accountability.

Honest engagement is often uncomfortable. We hear and speak unpleasant truths. Yet the *medrash* says that one who protests/reproves finds more *chen* than who elides the discomfort. According to the midrash, these real, if awkward, conversations are the essence of chen. True grace requires an investment in growth.

Bilaam's name is parsed by the Talmud[4] as B'li Am, free from people. As a quintessential outsider, Bilaam had a unique perspective on the people of Israel. Had he been willing to do the emotional labor of having the difficult conversations with them, he would have helped them be better aware of themselves and advance a more just coexistence.

Mishnah Avot[5] teaches that Bilaam is emblematic of the evil eye. He didn't view himself as part of the collective, nor did he feel responsible for anyone else. The Torah teaches that the proper perspective is to see people as worthy of effort and investment as part of humanity's development and evolution to a more perfect society. In doing so, we are partnering with God in the ongoing process of *naese adom*, "Let us make a person". Humanity is more idyllically formed when we work together to elevate each other towards communal perfection.

---

[4] Bavli Sanhedrin 105a.
[5] 5:19.

The *midrash*[6] observes the attitudinal difference that Moses and Bilaam have towards people. Biliam compares us to dust,[7] whereas Moses describes us as the stars in the sky.[8] While both dust and stars are too numerous to count, Moses's blessing reflects the aspirational reality that the closer we get to people, like stars, the greater they appear.

At a time when many people are becoming mobilized to protest racial violence, police brutality, and LGBTQ inequality, we must be careful not to fall into Bilaam's trap. We must expand beyond smooth slogans and superficial alliances and instead form deep coalitions based on relationship building and respectful dialogue. We must commit to working together with a deeper understanding of each other; listening tirelessly and consistently while devoutly showing up with a unifying love. Together, we can see one another more completely and stand up for each other more authentically, so that we may all be part of a more just world.

---

[6] Bemidbar Rabbah 2:12.

[7] Numbers 23:10.

[8] Deuteronomy 1:10.

Pinchas - Graceful Peace

לָכֵן, אֱמֹר: הִנְנִי נֹתֵן לוֹ אֶת-בְּרִיתִי, שָׁלוֹם.

Therefore say: Behold, I give him My covenant of peace.

Numbers 25:12

When trying to fix something, we can either address the consequences of the problem or its root cause. Pinchas witnessed a terrible sin that desecrated God's name. His response however, did not treat the ailment. By killing Zimri and Cozbi, he did away with the immediate symptoms of the sin, but he did not address the underlying issue that produced it.

This verse opens with "therefore" to highlight the cause and effect of Pinchas's actions. The Bal Haturim points out that this first word לָכֵן has the numerical value of measure for measure (מדה במדה), highlighting that God is responding to the previous event. However much appreciated his gesture was by God, it wasn't a lack of this particular action that necessitated the reaction. The letter "*Vuv*" in the Hebrew word for peace in this verse, שָׁלוֹם, is

broken[1] because Pinchas's response was deficient. It didn't
bring about a wholesome peace, allowing the individuals to
change and channel their focus to good, but simply
removed the perpetrators, and the potential to correct the
situation.[2]

The Midrash[3] explains that Pinchas eventually returns as
Elijah the Prophet. In that role he has a unique position in
ushering in the ultimate redemption; and with it a return to
the ideal. Malachi prophesied: "I will send the prophet
Elijah to you before the coming of the awesome day…He
shall reconcile parents with children and children with
their parents".[4] Pinchas also has a personal transformation
reflected through the letter "י" added to his name[5] so that
it reads פינחס; which is an anagram for חן פני, a face of
mercy.[6]

Perhaps one way to understand this strange consequence,
of rewarding violence with peace, is in acknowledging both
the pureness of Pinchas's passion for God,[7] and also just
how incompatible that way of being is for the world in
which we live. Although he is already prepared and

---

[1] Bavli Kiddushin 66b.
[2] L'horos Nossan.
[3] Yalkut Shimoni 771.
[4] 3: 23-24.
[5] Zohar 3 213b.
[6] Ahavas Shalom.
[7] R' Sternbuch writes that jealousy is different because the whole
mitzvah is intention.

operating for a future world of exacting and eternal good, his corrective task now is not to react, but to restore.

This balance of presence and absence, body and spirit, is reflected in the angelic aspect of nothingness, אין -ein, and the very human component of substance יש - eish.[8] These words together יש ואין have the same numerical value as the word "shalom" שלום.[9] This is the covenant of peace, to hold both the spiritual and physical together in harmony, without any tendencies towards evil.[10]

There is an interesting connection, through this *vuv hachebor*, the conjunction "and", between Jacob and Elijah. Rashi[11] explains that we find five places in Scripture where Jacob's name, יעקב, is written plene (יעקוב) and the name אליהו is also written defectively in five places. This suggests that Jacob — as it were — took one letter of Elijah's name as a pledge that at some future time he should come and proclaim the good tidings of his descendants' redemption.[12]

Although Elijah won't come on the Sabbath,[13] מִפְּנֵי הַטּוֹרַח - because of the inconvenience, Pinchas is understood to be already operating in Shabbat mode. He is the seventh generation after Jacob, and represents an embodiment of

---

[8] Torahs HaRemez.

[9] עד בכלל.

[10] Alshech quoted by Tiul B'Pardes.
[11] Vayikra 26:42.
[12] Midrash חסירות ויתירות.
[13] Bavli Eruvin 43b.

Shabat.[14] According to the early mystical work, Sefer
Yetzira, the letter "ת" governs over "חן" - grace and
corresponds to Shabbat. Those three letters form the word
חתן, groom, and have the same numerical value as the
word "חמתי" - "my anger"[15] in the previous verse;[16]
teaching that gracefulness is also a cure for anger.

This is part of the inheritance of Jacob as the Prophet
Isaiah[17] taught: וְקָרָ֫אתָ לַשַּׁבָּ֣ת עֹ֑נֶג ... והנחלתיך נַחֲלַ֫ת יַעֲקֹ֣ב
אָבִ֔יךָ - If you call the shabbat a delight...I will give you the
heritage of your father Jacob."[18] The gift of shabbat is also
called "shalom",[19] because it can transport us to that place
of goodness and blessing.

Rashi[20] also observes a reciprocity "like a person who
shows graciousness and friendliness to one who has done
them kindness". This type of chein reminds us that we
must try to focus our response in generative ways that
bring more goodness and perfection to the world.

---

[14] Rabanue B'Chaya.
[15] Chamra Tava.
[16] 25:11.
[17] 58:13-14.
[18] נַחֲלַ֫ת יַעֲקֹ֣ב אָבִ֔יךָ = על בְּנֵי־יִשְׂרָאֵל.
[19] Zohar 3: 176b.
[20] Numbers 25:12.

Mattos - Graceful Anger

וַיִּקְצֹף מֹשֶׁה, עַל פְּקוּדֵי הֶחָיִל, שָׂרֵי הָאֲלָפִים וְשָׂרֵי הַמֵּאוֹת,
הַבָּאִים מִצְּבָא הַמִּלְחָמָה.

Moses was angry with the commanders of the army, the officers of the thousands and officers of the hundreds, who came from the legion of the battle.

Numbers 31:14

The Talmud[1] posits in the name of Reish Lakish: "Any person who becomes angry, if they are a Torah scholar, their wisdom departs, and if they are a prophet, their prophecy departs." It offers as support, this incident with Moshe and the subsequent substitution in verse 21: "And Elazar the Priest said to the men of war who went to the battle 'This is the statute of the law, which the Lord commanded Moses'."

---

[1] Pesachim 66b.

174

We find many cautionary notes about anger from the rabbis - "Whoever get angry it is as if they are serving idols[2]", "Anyone who gets angry, (at that moment) even the Divine Presence is not important to them[3]", and on a positive note: "God loves the ones who don't get angry[4]".

Witnessing someone in a fit of anger is never pleasant or graceful. In fact, tradition teaches that when a person is overcome with anger, an aspect of the Divine Spirit leaves them[5] and with it, God's gift of grace. The Zohar explains that while sometimes it is necessary to present as angry, as a form of protest or communication, it must be controlled and limited to an external projection.

The Yismach Moshe[6] understand this to be the meaning of טוֹב כַּעַס מִשְּׂחֹק כִּי־בְרֹעַ פָּנִים יִיטַב לֵב "Anger is better than gaiety, for though the face is sad, the heart may be glad".[7] Meaning that the only time that anger is good is when a person is still able to be balanced with happiness on the inside.

This is alluded to in the concealed part of the Hebrew word for anger "כעס" / ka'as. The three letters, that form the word, are spelled: כ"ף עי"ן סמ"ך . The five letters that remain, (i.e. that are part of the vocalizations of each letter) and are not revealed in the conventional spelling, form the

[2] Zohar 3:179a.
[3] Nedarim 22b.
[4] Pesachim 113b.
[5] בזוהר הקדוש (ח"ג קע"ט ע"א).
[6] Ki Teitzei 12:11.
[7] Ecclesiastes 7:3.

word "פניכם" meaning face. If the perception of anger is truly external, than the פנים, the internal essence of holiness remains. However, if a person is consumed by it, then the impurity of those negative forces are also internalized.[8]

The Maharsha explains that one's loss of wisdom, due to anger, is simply the consequence of the distance to the source of the wisdom that is generated by moving away from the consciousness of God's presence. A person gets angry when something appears to them to be bad, only to the extent that they believe that God is not overseeing it all.[9]

In his writings on anger, the Maharal[10] elaborates on the connection between getting angry and forgetting the Torah that one has learned. He says about our relationship with God and God's attribute of being slow to anger: "one who is similar is loved by one who is similar". In getting angry, one is overly influenced by the physical world and is choosing to be governed in a physical and material plane. In doing so, one is prioritizing the superficial over one's intellect and spiritual domain and consequently, the power of that true knowledge is diminished as a person becomes less "God like".

It has been observed[11] that this principle connects two teachings from the great Tanna, Rabbi Eliezer ben

---

[8] Ben Yehoyada Pesachim 66b.
[9] Tannya Egeres Hakodesh 25.
[10] Netiv Hakas 1:3.
[11] Halekach V'halebuv.

Hyrcanus. Rabbi Yochanan said about his retention of Torah: "Rabbi Eliezer ben Hyrcanus is a plastered cistern which loses not a drop".[12] And a couple of mishnayos later we are taught in his name: "וְאַל תְּהִי נוֹחַ לִכְעֹס don't be quickly provoked to anger".

This can be easier said than done. Reb Yisroel Salent, the founder of the modern mussar movement, acknowledges that some people are born with an inherited proclivity to anger.[13] He also famously taught that it is harder to change one negative character trait than it is to study the entire Talmud! It is particularly because it is so difficult, however, that additional thought and effort must be applied to this struggle.

Rabbi Eliezer's teaching about anger is sandwiched between two other teachings: " יְהִי כְבוֹד חֲבֵרְךָ חָבִיב עָלֶיךָ וְשׁוּב יוֹם אֶחָד לִפְנֵי מִיתָתְךָ and כְּשֶׁלָּךְ - "Let the honor of your friend be as dear to you as your own" and "repent one day before your death". Perhaps, when we are triggered to anger, if we reflect on the broader context of what is really important in life, and remind ourselves how anger can damage our relationships with others, God, and ourselves, we can overcome the urge to lose ourselves in the moment.

---

[12] Pirkei Avos 2:8.
[13] Lev Eliyahu.

Masei - Graceful Strategies

וַיַּעַל אַהֲרֹן הַכֹּהֵן אֶל-הֹר הָהָר, עַל-פִּי יְהוָה--וַיָּמָת שָׁם: בִּשְׁנַת הָאַרְבָּעִים, לְצֵאת בְּנֵי-יִשְׂרָאֵל מֵאֶרֶץ מִצְרַיִם, בַּחֹדֶשׁ הַחֲמִישִׁי, בְּאֶחָד לַחֹדֶשׁ.

And Aharon, the Kohen, went up to Mount Hor by the mouth of Hashem and died there, in the fortieth year after the Children of Israel went forth from the land of Egypt, in the fifth month on the first of the month.

Numbers 33:38

Aharon, the great lover and pursuer of peace,[1] dies on Rosh Chodesh Av. This is the only time in the entire Torah where we are told the exact date of a person's death. The great loss and mourning the people experienced because of their closeness to him made the date noteworthy, and established it until this day as one of deep

---

[1] Avos 1:12.

sadness. As the Talmud[2] teaches: when the month of Av enters, we decrease our joy - מִשֶׁנִּכְנַס אָב מְמַעֲטִין בְּשִׂמְחָה.

What made people feel so connected to Aharon?[3] The Rabbis explain[4] that we all share the same source of our soul, and organically all of the fragments want to reunify and come together but our physicality, egos, and negative character traits often keep us separated. Aharon's great love for others and purity of soul, allowed people to experience a clarity of communal responsibility such that running after peace became the natural consequence.[5]

He also modeled how we should be in our relationship with God. The Jerusalem Talmud observes that there are 123 times in Hallel that we answer Hallelujah - praise is God; corresponding to the years of Aharon's life.[6] The Hebrew word for "year" - שנה - *shana*, is a language of change שנוי - *shenui* and the 123 years of Aron's life reflect these 123 different approaches that Aharon offered us to connect to God in Hallel. The Rabbis[7] contrast Moses' work of bringing God down to this world, to his brother Aharon's focus of elevating this world to God. This also parallels Moshe being compared[8] to the shabbos and Aharon to the new month.

---

[2] Bavli Tannis 29a.

[3] See Tam V'das.

[4] See M'eir Enie Chachamim on 79 in Nessuin/Lekutim.

[5] Chapter 16:12.

[6] See also Mishneh Torah Chanukah Purim 3:12.

[7] Zohar 3:53b and Likutei Maamarim.

[8] Sefas Emes 659.

The month of *Av*, in addition to being the saddest month of the year, also has an aspect of paternal love, as the word literally means father. One understanding of why Aharon's death is repeated here, although it is recounted first in great detail in *Parshas Chukas*, is that this *Parsha's* focus on traveling is a harbinger for our many stops in exile after the Temples are destroyed, both on the ninth of *Av*.[9]

Although God's house has been destroyed, that doesn't mean that we can't still all be a family. The Talmud[10] relates that the angels ask God how God can bestow favor on Israel, "[11]יִשָּׂא ה׳ פָּנָיו אֵלֶיךָ" after the Torah prohibits a father from showing favor.[12] The Talmud explains that because the people of Israel put in extra effort to do what is pleasing to God, it is only natural that God bestows favor upon Israel. The Munkatcher Rebbe[13] understands God's explanation to the angels as justifiable because we serve God out of love, the way a child fulfills the request of a parent. God is simply reciprocating that love in blessing us with it.

This is also reflected in the relationship we have with each other as siblings. The blessings that Aharon and his sons are commanded to give over to the Children of Israel, although in the singular, are introduced with the word "להם" - them.[14] Being unified as one, is what allows us to

---

[9] See Noam Magadim and Megali Amukos.
[10] Berachos 20b.
[11] Numbers 6:26.
[12] Deuteronomy 10:17.
[13] Alos Shabbos on Chodesh Tishrei.
[14] Numbers 6:23.

be worthy of the blessings.[15] This is the advice that the *medresh* gives us:[16] be graceful to each other חוֹנְנִים זֶה אֶת זֶה, to merit a peaceful coexistence.

Birkas Kohanim, the blessings that we are to receive from the Priests, introduces and frames the concluding blessing in the morning prayer of *Shemone Esre*:[17] "Grant peace, goodness, and blessing, grace...Bless us, our Father, all of us as one...". The *medresh*, exploring this aspect of grace, understands חן as wisdom, as we find in the blessing of אַתָּה חוֹנֵן לְאָדָם דֵּעַת - You grace a person with knowledge.[18] Aharon demonstrated profound wisdom and creativity in bringing peace and harmony between people, which is a prerequisite for redemption.

The Talmud[19] relates some of his motivational speeches to inspire couples, and individuals, to put in more effort to achieve peaceful relationships. As an indicator of his success there were eighty thousand young men named "Aaron" who followed Aaron's bier. They were the sons of those who were born because their parents had received marital advice from Aharon that brought them closer together. When we work on our love for humanity, pursuing peace comes naturally.

---

[15] Yetiv Lev.
[16] Bamidbar Rabbah 11:6.
[17] Bavli Megillah 18a.
[18] See Rav Simshon Refael Hirsch.
[19] Kallah Rabasi 3:4.

Sefer Devarim

Devarim - Graceful Speech

אֵלֶּה הַדְּבָרִים, אֲשֶׁר דִּבֶּר מֹשֶׁה אֶל-כָּל-יִשְׂרָאֵל, בְּעֵבֶר, הַיַּרְדֵּן: בַּמִּדְבָּר בָּעֲרָבָה מוֹל סוּף בֵּין-פָּארָן וּבֵין-תֹּפֶל, וְלָבָן וַחֲצֵרֹת–וְדִי זָהָב

These are the words that Moses spoke to all of Israel, across the Jordan, in the wilderness, in the Plain, opposite the Sea of Reeds, between Paran and Tophel and Laban, and Hazeroth and Di-zahab.

Deuteronomy 1:1

The book of Deuteronomy consists almost entirely of one exceedingly long speech delivered by Moses at the end of his life. The speech is so long that *Midrash Tanchuma* reports the Israelites saying, "Yesterday you said 'I'm not a man of words", and now you have SO much to say!"[1]

---

[1] Tanchuma 2.

The people listen to all of Moses' words. And as we read
Deuteronomy between now and Simchat Torah, we listen
as well. Moses does have a lot to say, and much of it is a
rebuke to the Israelites for their misbehavior during the
previous forty years. In our own time of great division and
non-communication, we can learn a lot from Moses'
unifying final words.

Moses' wordiness here appears out of character. In Egypt,
Aaron was the talker and Moses described himself as
having sealed lips (*aral sefatayim*). Yet over the course of
their journey through the wilderness, Aaron has learned to
be silent[2] and Moses has learned to speak. Rashi, on the
famous verse in Ecclesiastes[3] "there is a time to be silent
and a time to talk," references Aaron and Moses, in that
order. Each leader was able to expand beyond their natural
tendency when the time called for it.

Moses' speech begins on the first day of the month of
Shvat, just 36 days before his death.[4] Deuteronomy, the
fifth book in the Pentateuch, is called the *Mishnah Torah* by
the Rabbis. It's name, משנה, can be parsed שנה 'מ – forty
years. This marks the fact that 40 years have passed since
Moses received the Torah at Sinai, and the children of
Israel have been wandering in the wilderness for 40 years.
It also alludes to the 40 generations from Moshe to Rebbe

---

[2] Leviticus 10:3.
[3] 3:7.

[4] אלה = ל"ו.

Yehudah HaNassi, who redacts the Mishna that becomes the basis of our Talmud.[5]

The letter מ is also the first and last letter of the Oral Law. The first mishnah in the first tractate begins with the word מאימתי and the last word of the last tractate ends with the word שלום. (*me'amatai* and *shalom*). The two מ's together have the numerical value of 80 which corresponds to the Hebrew letter פ – peh, the mouth. This book is understood as the Torah *Sheba'al Peh*, the Oral Torah, in that Moshe is teaching the Divine word differently than in the first four books.[6] (Notably, in his retelling, some things are different than the first time around.)

Just as it was necessary for everyone to be united by the revelation at Sinai, here also it is essential for the community to be unified in hearing Moses' words. Rav Wolfson in his work *Emunat Atich* explains that all of Israel needed to be present at the same time, not just to hear Moses, but also to teach and learn from each other.[7] The letter ל / lamed appears at the end of each word in the phrase אל כל ישראל, (al kol Yisrael, "to all of Israel") and that letter ל is the root of the word לימוד / limud, meaning learning.

---

[5] Megaleh Amukos 246.
[6] Zohar Genesis 28:10.
[7] This is reflected in talmudic discussion about the proximity of teaching; even though some don't learn from the juxtaposition of verses, in the first four books, here they do.

Today we often place ourselves in siloed, self-selected groups with the goal of having easy conversations with like-minded people. In contrast, Moses gathers all of the people, all together, for a difficult conversation. Rashi, citing the Sifrei, explains why it is crucial that everyone be present at the same time: if some folks were in the marketplace during Moses' speech they would claim that had they been there, they could have refuted Moses. Moses speaks to everyone, engaging them with an opportunity for each individual to disagree and speak up if they choose.

The Zohar[8] attributes Moshe's success to his *chein* (grace) and connects him to the verse[9] "grace is poured upon your lips". The distinction between lips and speech is significant. The mystics[10] observe five distinct body parts integral to speech: the (1) throat, (2) palate, (3) tongue, (4) teeth, and (5) lips. Of the 22 letters of the Hebrew Alphabet, only 4 letter sounds are articulated by the lips.[11]

The Sefas Emes notes that lips are unusual in that they serve two speech functions. They both create sound, and prevent sound from leaving the mouth. Moshe uses his lips expertly. He speaks when he has something to say and is silent when he does not.

The Sefas Emes[12] also understands the two lips as working together. He says the lips allude to Moses and Aaron; and

---

[8] Parshas Bo.
[9] Psalms 45:3.
[10] Sefer Yetzirah 2:3.

[11] בומ"פ.

[12] Succos 654-6.

later, Hillel and Shammai. The two lips also represent different attributes. Silence is *din* (judgement) and talking is *rachamim* (mercy). The Written Torah represents strictness of the law, while the Oral Torah represents mercy and compassion.[13]

Compassionate speech doesn't mean indulging in one's own desire to talk, but rather creating opportunities for people to truly hear what needs to be said. Moses' authenticity of being, reliability of presence, and consistency of selflessness, allow the words that come from his heart to enter the hearts of others. Like Moses, we must lead with love, and learn from each other.

---

[13] עיין ספר הזכות: לא איש דברים אנכי ס"ת שמאי, הוא יהיה לך לפה ר"ת הילל.

Va'eschanan - Graceful Prayer

וָאֶתְחַנַּן, אֶל-יְהוָה, בָּעֵת הַהִוא, לֵאמֹר.

I implored Hashem, at that time, saying.

Deuteronomy 3:23

The prophet[1] charges us to "Rend your hearts rather than your garments... for God is gracious and compassionate". This is the prooftext that is used to support R' Shimon's teaching that prayer shouldn't be fixed, but that we should approach the Omnipresent from a stance of supplication and grace - אַל תַּעַשׂ תְּפִלָּתְךָ קֶבַע, אֶלָּא רַחֲמִים וְתַחֲנוּנִים לִפְנֵי הַמָּקוֹם.

This type of prayer, known as the service of the heart,[2] is seen as a consolation for our loss and mourning of the Temple.[3] Although we are not able to bring *korbanos* -

<hr>

[1] Joel 2:13.
[2] Bavli Tanis 2a.
[3] Halekach V'halebuv.

187

sacrifices, we are still able to achieve that closeness - *kiruv* - through attaching ourselves to God as the source of good.[4] The comfort that we receive this Shabbos[5] by reading the Haftorah of Nachamu Nachamu Ami, (*Take comfort, take comfort my people*) also reflects the charge of the prophet to open our hearts so we can change the brokenness of the world and fill it with pleasure from the Divine.

"I implore" is one the ten expressions of prayer,[6] and tradition teaches that even though Moshe was told that he wasn't going to be able to cross the Jordan into Israel, he still prayed[7] and offered five hundred and fifteen supplications,[8] corresponding to the numerical value of the word "V'eschannan".[9] The *medresh*[10] uses this as the model to teach future generations to pray during difficult times.

One of the distinguishing characteristics of this particular form of prayer is the awareness of the lack of entitlement to be answered. Rashi teaches that all forms of the word "חנון" always mean "a gift for free" and the Maharal points out the root of these forms is *chein*, grace.[11] The Rabbis[12] explain that it isn't just framing one's prayer without the expectation of feeling that the request is due, but an

---

[4] Rabanu Yona.
[5] Shabbos is also see as a gift and a comfort see Sichos Kodesh.
[6] Sifrei.
[7] Prayer - תפלה also equals 515.
[8] Also the same value as שירה song - Bal Haturim.
[9] Midrash Rabbah 11:1.
[10] Midrash Rabbah 2:6.
[11] ואתחנן אין חנון בכל מקום וכו'. פירוש "ואתחנן" הוא לשון חנם, כי 'חנם' שרשו 'חנן'.
[12] Shiurim B'Tefilah p. 110.

internal recognition of how indebted we are to God for all of the good that we have received.[13]

God's mercy and kindness are limitless and offering one's request from that heart space allows for greater authenticity, connection, and intimacy. The *medresh* records that when Moses ascended into heaven, he saw a great storage house and asked God, "Whom is this for?" God answers, "For those who toil in learning Torah." Moshe then sees another enormous warehouse and asks the same question to which G-d responds, "It is for those who do acts of kindness." This continues until Moshe comes across a warehouse that has no boundaries and God answers him "this is the one of free gifts", and this, the *medresh* continues, is the supplication of *V'eschanan*.

When we come to God to make a request, with a sense of entitlement, there is a reasonable evaluation process to determine if we are really worthy of our ask being fulfilled. We avoid this process when we acknowledge God's generosity and kindness beyond anything we might feel we have coming to us.

This is also true in our interpersonal relationships. When we start keeping track of how much others have done for us as the indicator of how we will treat them, we limit our own expressions of goodness, and will invariably feel like we have received less than we deserve.

---

[13] Kli Yakar

Shabbos is described[14] by God, to Moses, as "a good gift" and according to the mystical tradition[15] is the "time" (בְּעֵת הַהִוא) referenced in Moses's prayer. The Zohar[16] observes that the generational (דורותם) covenant of the Shabbat is spelled with a deficiency of the letter "vuv" forming the word for "dwelling" *dirah*. This "vuv", the sixth letter of the Hebrew Alphabet, makes an appearance in the beginning of "*V'eschanan*" as an allusion to the six days of the week where we work[17] and request, based on that effort. However, the Shabbat is the day of rest and one where we do not tally up what we deserve and what we desire. It is an invitation to accept blessings, comfort, and nourishment by just being, while also finding comfort in our ability to partner with God in the formation and creation of a better world.

---

[14] Bavli Shabbos 10b.

[15] Zohar 2 88b also see Ahavat Shalom.

[16] Zohar 3:238b לְדֹרוֹתָם, לְדֹרתָם חָסֵר, לְשׁוֹן דִּירָה.

[17] Sichos Kodesh.

Eikev- Graceful Gratitude

וְאָכַלְתָּ, וְשָׂבָעְתָּ--וּבֵרַכְתָּ אֶת-יְקוָק אֱלֹקיךָ, עַל-הָאָרֶץ הַטֹּבָה
אֲשֶׁר נָתַן-לָךְ.

You will eat and you will be satisfied and you will bless
Hashem, your God, for the good land that God gave you.

Deuteronomy 8:10

Although the blessing over bread simply acknowledges
"Blessed is the One who delivers bread from earth -
Hamotzi Lechem Min Haaretz", the Talmud[1] identifies
eleven distinct acts of labor that were necessary for Adam
to first produce bread. The understatedness of the
declaration invites us to develop a greater appreciation for
so many of the essential benefits that we take for granted.

Food, in general, is something that many struggle with to
find a healthy balance of intake and intention. For this
reason, the word *lechem* לחם is related to *milchama* מלחמה

---

[1] Bavli Berachot 58a.

war.[2] The Torah also positions the potential for food to either bring us closer or further away from God.[3] It is formulated by the Vilnia Goan as: "If we are meritorious then we eat the food, if not, the food consumes us."[4] Conceptualizing eating as a tool and opportunity is helpful in framing and elevating the experience.

In the Code of Jewish Law[5] we are instructed to orient even mundane actions for the sake of Heaven. The Rabbis[6] teach that it is a higher act to eat with intention, than to fast with the same thoughtfulness. King Solomon[7] writes: מַה־יָּפִית וּמַה־נָּעַמְתְּ אַהֲבָה בַּתַּעֲנוּגִים - How fair you are, how beautiful! O Love, with all its rapture!". Its deeper meaning is that love for God is more recognizable through enjoying this world than by refraining from it. When we realize the limitations of an exclusively physical engagement, it becomes more attractive to embrace and enhance the experience through the limitless spiritual components.

An easy ritual to accustom ourselves to is the gratitude practice of making a blessing over the food that we are fortunate to receive. The first blessing of the grace after meals was established by Moses when the *manna* first fell from heaven.[8] Although "bread from the earth" is hardly

---

[2] Zohar 3:272a.
[3] Deuteronomy 31:20.
[4] Aderes Eliyahu.
[5] Orach Chaim 231:1.
[6] Igeres Hatuil Cheleck HaPsat B'shem R' Tzodok.
[7] Song of Songs 7:7.
[8] Bavli Berachot 48b.

relatable to *manna* from heaven, perhaps it helps us contextualize our effort and work in a partnership with the miraculous when we realize that everything good in this physical world has its source in Heaven.[9]

Constantly acknowledging the Source of All Blessing throughout the day connects us to God. Reb Tzadok[10] shares that the Mishna's first tractate is called "Blessings" because it is the root of the entire Torah. The Talmud warns of the negative consequences of benefiting from the world without acknowledging those benefits with a blessing.

כָּל הַנֶּהֱנֶה מִן הָעוֹלָם הַזֶּה בְּלֹא
בְּרָכָה כְּאִילּוּ גּוֹזֵל לְהַקָּדוֹשׁ בָּרוּךְ
הוּא וּכְנֶסֶת יִשְׂרָאֵל

Whoever benefits from this
world, without offering a
blessing, it is as if they have
stolen from God and the Nation
of Israel.

It is understandable to equate making a blessing with asking permission, the way the Talmud[11] resolves the apparent contradicting verses of "The earth and all it contains is the Lord's,"[12] and "The heavens are the Lord's

---

9 See Tzidkas Hatzadik 191.
10 Tzidkas HaTzadik 232.
11 Bavli Berachot 35a.
12 Psalms 24:1.

and the earth, God has given over to people".[13] The commentaries suggest that a lack of gratitude causes the dissolution of society and is therefore also an act of thievery against the Jewish people.[14]

The first line of the benediction hints at a structure of Divine motivation in response to our collective attitude to God:

הַזָּן אֶת־הָעוֹלָם כֻּלּוֹ בְּטוּבוֹ בְּחֵן
בְּחֶסֶד וּבְרַחֲמִים

> Who nourishes the entire world
> with goodness, with grace, with
> kindness, and with mercy."

God is good, and our ability to receive that goodness is determined by our actions. Grace, kindness, and mercy represent three distinct approaches along a spectrum of the ways in which God provides for us[15] - the more worthy, the more grace, the less worthy the more need for mercy.

Being satiated isn't a function of how much we have consumed, but how we feel about what we have.[16] The verse focuses on the goodness of the land to teach us that

---

[13] Psalms 115:16.
[14] See Beurim V'Hanhagos.
[15] Siddur Ohr HaChama.
[16] Rav Moshe Dovid Velli.

gratitude is a crucial condition for enjoying a good life in God's good land.

Re'eh - Graceful Faith

רְאֵה, אָנֹכִי נֹתֵן לִפְנֵיכֶם--הַיּוֹם: בְּרָכָה, וּקְלָלָה.

See, I place before you today a blessing and a curse.

Deuteronomy 11:26

When the world was being created, all of the letters came before God wanting to be chosen to be the first in the Torah,[1] understood as the blueprint for creation.[2] God responded to each one and decided to begin with the second letter of the Hebrew Alphabet, *bet*, because it represents *bracha* blessing, while the *aleph*, the first letter, has a connection to *arrur* - curse. In consolation, the *aleph* is told that it will find its place beginning the Ten Commandments with the word *Anochi* "I".

The Baal HaTurim explains the first two words in this verse, *re'eh anochie*, as "you saw the Ten Commandments

---

[1] Zohar 1:205b.
[2] Zohar 2:161a.

that begin with the word *Anochi*". This week's parsha is always read either on the Shabbat of Rosh Chodesh Ellul, or the one before, Shabbat Mevarchim, primarily because it highlights the empowerment that comes with the agency to make choices.[3] It also reminds us that we are held responsible for those decisions, because we have the ability to choose them.

The first word, *re'eh*, also alludes to the seeing of the sounds[4] at Mt. Sinai.[5] Although society has accepted the saying "that seeing is believing", our rabbis[6] teach the opposite; if you see something, you no longer need to believe. The threshold of faith for each of us is different and often fluid, but as a people we have it rooted in the exodus of Egypt and the giving of the Torah at Mt. Sinai.[7] It is perhaps for that reason the "seeing" here is in the singular, while "you" is in the plural. Although the point of our free will is person and moment specific, the working mechanism of improving who we are is the same, and requires a lot of faith.

Maimonides writes that we are meant to see the world completely balanced, between good and evil, and our very next act will tip the scales in one direction or the other.[8] An additional aspect of having faith in ourselves is that we

---

[3] Olas Shabbos .

[4] Exodus 20:15.

[5] Ahavas Shalom p. 431.

[6] Divrie Chaim.

[7] Yaytiv Lev p. 70.

[8] Hilchos Teshuva 3:4.

must believe that we have an impact on the world around us.

Rosh Chodesh Elul reminds us that the choice to serve the Golden Calf forced the breaking of the first set of Tablets. It was on that day that Moses went back up the mountain to receive the second set[9] to deliver on Yom Kippur, the Day of Atonement. One of the ways that we prepare during this month is by reciting Psalms 27, twice daily. In verse thirteen King David hints to the faith we must have in being able to change our ways to come closer to God. He writes:

$$\text{לוּלֵא הֶאֱמַנְתִּי לִרְאוֹת בְּטוּב־ה'...}$$

> Had I not trusted that I would see the goodness of Hashem.

The rabbis observe that the first word of the verse is an anagram for this month of Elul. It alludes to the faith we have knowing that when I am for my Beloved, that my Beloved is for me. We put ourselves out there, and God reciprocates אני לדודי ודודי לי.[10]

As we approach Rosh Hashana, the birthday of the world, we recall that it is us that makes this world worthy of celebration. It is the Godly within us that makes us intrinsically holy and imbues us with the power to manifest that goodness to the world. Adam is formed *min haadama*

---

[9] Tur, Orach Chaim 581.
[10] Song of Songs 6:3.

from the ground, but it is also a language of comparison or likeness as אֶדַּמֶּה לְעֶלְיוֹן I will match the Most High.[11]

Our similarity to God is what holds us accountable to act Godly, and reflect God's grace. As Abba Shaul taught:[12] אַבָּא שָׁאוּל אוֹמֵר: "וְאַנְוֵהוּ" — הֱוֵי דוֹמֶה לוֹ, מָה הוּא חַנּוּן וְרַחוּם — אַף אַתָּה הֱיֵה חַנּוּן וְרַחוּם. We should be like God - just as God is graceful and compassionate, so too should we be graceful and compassionate. A person coming together in this way is alluded to in the numerical value of אחד, meaning the One God, = 13, and אדם person = 45, equalling 58 the value of חן - chein.[13]

Through the learning of Torah we are able to channel the potential energy of curse into blessing by experiencing God's holiness, similar to what occurred at Mt. Sinai. The Talmud[14] sees the Divine revelation of "Anochi" as continuing through the study of Torah itself: "אָנֹכִי", נוֹטְרִיקוֹן: אֲנָא נַפְשִׁי כְּתָבִית יְהָבִית - "Anochi is an acronym for I, my soul, in written form I gave." This is explained by the Slonimer Rebbe[15] as if the soul of God is wrapped up in the words of Torah and can be found and attached to through its learning.

The letter Aleph, when spelled out, is an anagram for wonderment - פלא.[16] When we reflect on the source of our

---

[11] Isaiah 14:14.
[12] Bavli Shabbat 133b.
[13] Ben Yehoyada sukkah 56b.
[14] Bavli Shabbat 105a.
[15] Nesivos Shalom Eikev.
[16] Bilvavi Mishkan Evneh on Path of the Just.

faith; the miraculous nature of God's oneness, being, and creating, we can grow our belief in the power of our own actions as well to ensure a dominant expression of blessing.

Shoftim - Graceful Justice

צֶדֶק צֶדֶק, תִּרְדֹּף--לְמַעַן תִּחְיֶה וְיָרַשְׁתָּ אֶת-הָאָרֶץ, אֲשֶׁר-יְקוָק אֱלֹקיךָ נֹתֵן לָךְ.

Justice, justice shall you pursue, so that you will live and take possession of the land that Hashem, your God, gives you.

Deuteronomy 16:20

Justice can never be about just us! The verse repeats the word "justice" to teach that an individualized, selective, or singular justice for oneself is not what we should be pursuing.[1] "רדף" to pursue, is an anagram for פרד - separation.[2] We must ensure that we seek justice for others as we would for ourselves, without any separation within humanity.

---

[1] Chida.
[2] Toras HaRemez.

The rabbis acknowledge that often there are competing interests and limited resources. One person's accessibility might come at the expense of another's. The Talmud also sees the process of compromise as a communal form of justice, framing the repetition as אחד לדין ואחד לפשרה, whether a strict judgment or a settlement agreement.[3]

Two situations are given as examples[4] of this principle. Different boats are traveling on the river where if both of them attempt to pass, both of them sink, but if they take turns and one goes after the other, both of them can pass. Similarly, where there are two camels who are ascending a narrow steep path, if both of them attempt to ascend simultaneously, both of them fall. However, if they ascend one after the other, both of them have safe passage. Despite the fact that these solutions seem obvious, convincing people to work together and to make concessions to each other can be exceedingly difficult.

King Solomon taught[5] "שֶׂכֶל־טוֹב יִתֶּן־חֵן וְדֶרֶךְ בֹּגְדִים אֵיתָן - Good sense provides grace, but the way of the faithless is harsh." Rashi[6] explains that it is harsh for the person, without good sense, and also for others. Self-centeredness displaces thoughtfulness, and even common sense. However the opposite is also true. When we are forgiving, in order to prioritize the needs of another, then God

---

[3] Bavli Sanhedrin 32b.
[4] See Ben Yehoyada for why both are necessary.
[5] Proverbs 13:15.

[6] קשה לו ולאחרים.

reciprocates and is חַנּוּן הַמַּרְבֶּה לִסְלוֹחַ - even more forgiving of us with grace.

Although it is usually the purview of the rabbis to make fences, we find an additional charge in the Torah to take preparatory and preventive actions:[7] "מִדְּבַר־שֶׁקֶר תִּרְחָק - from a falsehood distance yourself".[8] The Sefas Emes[9] understands the pursuit of truth and justice to be one and the same. Distancing from lies and coming closer to the truth, he says, is the foundation of everything.

One must be passionate about this endeavor and never be complacent. The rabbis teach that if we ever see ourselves as righteous enough (צדק), we will stop working for more (צדק).[10] This is perhaps reflected in the numerical value of צדק"seeking" equalling two times - חפש[11].[12]

Recognizing the complexity of coexistence provides an opportunity to come together, not simply to overcome obstacles, but to use the challenges themselves as an opportunity to increase unity. This might be the space between the problem solving faculty of *sechel* common sense, and *sechel tov*, a common sense that expands into the common good.

---

[7] HaRav M'Peshischa.
[8] Exodus 23:7.
[9] 639.
[10] Meor V'shemesh.
[11] 388.
[12] 194.

A humorous parable is offered by Rabbi Shimon bar Yochai[13] to demonstrate the absurdity of extreme self focus: A group of people were traveling on a ship when one of them tooks a drill and started drilling a hole in the boat by his feet. The others start protesting and ask "What are you doing?!" He replied: "What do you care? Is this not underneath my area that I am drilling?!" They respond: "But the water will rise and flood us all on this ship." The *medresh* concludes by reading this into the story of Job: [14] "If indeed I have erred, my error remains with me." But his friends said to him: "He adds transgression to his sin; he extends it among us."[15]

When we orient ourselves to doing good, we don't need to wait for something bad to happen to activate our response. Another consequence of a communal focus is gaining access to the collective resources when our attitude produces a grace that invites others to contribute.[16] Only when we are being proactive for the wellbeing of others will we be worthy to live properly on God's property.

---

[13] Vayikra Rabbah 4:6.
[14] Job 19:4.
[15] Job 34:37.
[16] See Rav Mosh David Velli.

Ki Seitzei - Graceful Building

כִּי תִבְנֶה בַּיִת חָדָשׁ, וְעָשִׂיתָ מַעֲקֶה לְגַגֶּךָ; וְלֹא-תָשִׂים דָּמִים
בְּבֵיתֶךָ, כִּי-יִפֹּל הַנֹּפֵל מִמֶּנּוּ.

If you will build a new house, you shall make a fence for your roof, so that you will not place blood in your house if one who falls, falls from it.

Deuteronomy 22:8

Our bodies house our souls and this verse is understood as referring not only to a new physical home, but also to a newly repentant body. As we prepare for Rosh Hashana we are tasked with repairing the mistakes of the last year, and in doing so we are rebuilding ourselves and creating a new ideal home for our soul. Old habits are hard to break and our tradition encourages us to generate positive momentum, through good actions, as the easiest way to shift our routines in the right direction.

Just before the *mitzvah* of fencing in one's roof, we are taught of the commandment to send away a mother bird prior to taking her young. Rashi explains the juxtaposition

205

as "one mitzvah leads to another mitzvah". When we
habituate ourselves to doing good, it seems we are granted
more opportunities to advance that cause. "*Mitzvah*" is a
language of connectivity and brings us closer to God, the
source of all goodness, and also manifests the goodness of
our soul into this world. As an example, the Ramchal[1]
frames our ability to overcome laziness in relationship to
our recognition of how good God is to us. Being roused to
passionate acts of holiness is the natural consequence of
removing the obstacles to that awareness.

These commandments map our path of existence and
accompany us along the journey. The *medresh*[2] applies the
verse[3] "for they are an adornment/accompaniment (לוית)
of grace" to the mitzvah of building a fence on one's
parapet. King Solomon, the author of Proverbs, could
have simply stated that the Torah guides us on our way -
what role does grace play in it?

In the mystical tradition, a person's head corresponds to
God's Name[4], the *shem Havaya*[5] and is alluded to in the
fence, גג, also having a numerical value of 26.[6] Just as a
person on the top of a building needs protection from
falling, so too the Divine presence resting atop a person's
faculties also needs to be guarded.

---

[1] Mesilas Yesharim Chapter 8.
[2] Devarim Rabbah 6:3.
[3] Proverbs 1:9.

[4] עיין בהלקח והלבוב בשם המג"ע.
[5] י-ה-ו-ה.

[6] Ariz"l.

This natural resting place of the Divine was lost after the sin in the garden, but is restored through repentance. We now must be proactive in preserving this aspect of the *Alufo Shel Alom*, The One Source of the World, represented in the *aleph* א of Adam אדם. The letter א is made up of two yuds "י" and a vuv "ו", equalling 26.[7] The mystics read this verse as a warning to protect our holiness or risk losing the *aleph* and again descending "to have blood" - dam דם - adam without the *aleph*.[8]

The Medresh[9] tells the story about Adam's ability to name all of the animals, based on their essential identities. After proving his skillset, God asks Adam: "And what is my name"? Adam answers with the *Shem Havya* as it says אֲנִי יְקֹוָק הוּא שְׁמִי - I am Hashem, that is my name[10] - because it is what Adam called me. The *medresh* concludes by explaining that this name provides the condition for us to be in a relationship with God through the commandments.

This is the function of being guided by grace.[11] When we move with the intention of healing the brokenness of the world, we are presented with a Godly partnership to repair it all. King David writes[12] יְחָנֵּנוּ וִיבָרְכֵנוּ יָאֵר פָּנָיו אִתָּנוּ סֶלָה May God be gracious and bless us, may God illuminate

---

[7] Although sometimes with two "*vuv*".
[8] Ben Ish Chai Drashos.
[9] Tanchuma 8:1.
[10] Isaiah 42:8.
[11] Yativ Lev.
[12] Psalms 67:2.

God's countenance with us.[13] It has been observed[14] that God shines "with us" (אִתָּנוּ), not "on us". Grace is first given to us, and then we are blessed with the hidden light of the Torah[15] to renew our body and spirit.

---

[13] See the Chida for why the order is different from the priestly blessing.
[14] R' Shimshon Refael Hirsh.
[15] R' Shmuel Vosner.

Ki Savo - Graceful Inheritance

וְהָיָה, כִּי-תָבוֹא אֶל-הָאָרֶץ, אֲשֶׁר יְהוָה אֱלֹהֶיךָ, נֹתֵן לְךָ נַחֲלָה;
וִירִשְׁתָּהּ, וְיָשַׁבְתָּ בָּהּ.

It will be when you enter the land that Hashem, your God,
gives you as an inheritance, and you take possession, and
dwell, in it.

Deuteronomy 26:1

Like the Israelites in the wilderness, we have all inherited a
broken world in deep need of urgent repair. Each day
brings with it new tragedies to add to the ones that came
before. Our daily struggle to advance progress and healing,
feels like an embraceable holiness that is modeled by our
ancestors and tradition. It is dispiriting to know though,
that while today will end, the chaos and loss will naturally
continue tomorrow. The *medresh*[1] presents a different view
and categorizes this verse as a language of *simcha*. The
people are promised a land that will be healed and

---

[1] Vayikra Rabbah 11:7.

restored, an experience uniquely suited to erase the pain of the past.[2]

This verse introduces the commandment of bringing the first fruits to the Temple, a commandment which only applies in the Land of Israel. Yet the word "וְהָיָה" (it will be), implying joy,[3] doesn't introduce the subsequent two words, "כִּי-תָבוֹא" - (when you enter), where they appear in Leviticus 19:23 or in Numbers 15:2.[4] It seems this happiness, and obligation to bring the first fruits, strangely are only achieved once the land is settled, but not simply by entering it. Additionally, why does the verse seem to make a distinction between *Nachla* and *Yerusha*, ostensibly synonyms for inheritance?

The Ben Ish Chai offers an insight that provides a broader outlook for the framing of this verse. He observes that when King David describes the Land of Israel[5] he speaks of it in the plural: בְּאַרְצוֹת הַחַיִּים in the **lands** of the living. Quoting the mystical tradition,[6] the letter "ת", spelled "תו", alludes to Torah, תו-רה - that was received on הר -Mount Sinai.

We know the Torah has its geographical source in Israel, as the verse[7] testifies "For the Torah shall come forth

---

[2] See Ohr Hachaim Hakodesh who see is as a fulfillment of Psalm 126:2.

[3] והיה לשון שמחה Ohr Hachaim.

[4] Malbim.

[5] Psalms 116:9 see Rashi.

[6] קה"י בשם אותיות דרבי עקיבא.

[7] Isaiah 2:3.

from Zion" and this is the Lands of Israel that King David is referencing; ארצות - a Torah centric Israel. The Ben Ish Chai continues that the plurality of the lands, and the living - חיים - is created by the different layers and levels of the Torah, particularly the *Pardes*.[8] King Solomon writes[9]: כִּי לֶקַח טוֹב נָתַתִּי לָכֶם תּוֹרָתִי אֱל־תַּעֲזֹבוּ - for I give you good instruction...and the good - טוב - having a numerical valua of 17, multiplied by the four categories of the *Pardes*, equals the 68 of חיים, the living.

This is further alluded to in the word "תבוא" - when the Torah comes - תו בא, the land will be for you. Only when the land is settled in a way that supports the Torah's teachings will we be worthy of receiving the land that was promised to our ancestors. This is the inheritance that awaits us as a נחלה. It is the grace that is produced by the learning of Torah - חן לה that makes it a pleasant and peaceful gift from God. In the *medrash*[10] we find that the priestly blessing "ויחונך" is understood as connected to חינוך, education. The blessing means יחנך בתלמוד תורה to be blessed with grace through the study of Torah.[11]

The word "תבוא" can also be arranged to form the word for ancestors, אבות.[12] Rav Nosson Gestetner articulates the distinguishing feature of a *Yerusha* as being that which

---

[8] The Pshat, Remez, Dras, and Sod.
[9] Proverbs 4:2.
[10] Sifre Bamidbar 41.
[11] Also see Kol Bo 118.
[12] Bal Haturim also the 30 of כי is an allusion to the 30 minimum righteous people in Israel.

is inherited, as opposed to gifted.[13] Gifts are discretionary, whereas an inheritance is received regardless of merit. Like the Torah says about itself[14] תּוֹרָה צִוָּה־לָנוּ מֹשֶׁה מוֹרָשָׁה קְהִלַּת יַעֲקֹב - the heritage of the Congregation of Jacob.

The settling referenced here is a mindset that contributes to our ability to be happy. Ramchal[15] equates our capacity to recognize the temporary nature of being settled in this world, and the permanence of our spiritual existence, to living a happier life free from the worries that distract from our true inheritance - נחלה נחלת עולמים.[16]

Simcha (joy) has the same root as *somach*, to be supported.[17] When a person feels that God is taking care of them, how could they not be overwhelmed with happiness? The Rebbe Reb Zusha parses the morning blessing thanking God for "who provides me with all of my needs" - שֶׁעָשָׂה לִי כָּל־צָרְכִּי - as "everything that was provided for me, I need". Knowing that God loves us and understanding that it is that love which motives all of the commandments, causes us to be in relationship with God through joy. It is perhaps for that reason that we are warned later in the *parsha*[18] of the negative consequences of not operating out of *simcha*, because it is an indicator of one's lack of faith.

---

[13] L'horos Nosson.
[14] Deuteronomy 33:4.
[15] *Path of the Just* chapter 9.
[16] Zevachim 119b.
[17] *Emunas Aticha* volume 2.
[18] 28:47.

Bringing the first fruit offering requires the accompanying intention, and sensation, of gratitude for everything that has happened in the past until the present including explicit mentioning of the oppression and hardships.[19] Only when we are able to appreciate the Divine source of the land,[20] and the expectations of dwelling in it, will we be able to fulfill the words of King David's redemption of Zion[21] הַזֹּרְעִים בְּדִמְעָה בְּרִנָּה יִקְצֹרוּ - those who sow in tears shall reap with songs of joy.

---

[19] 26:3-10.
[20] See Bavli Sotah 47a.
[21] Psalm 126:5.

Nitzavim - Graceful Bar Mitzvah

רְאֵה נָתַתִּי לְפָנֶיךָ הַיּוֹם, אֶת-הַחַיִּים וְאֶת-הַטּוֹב, וְאֶת-הַמָּוֶת, וְאֶת-הָרָע.

See, I set before you this day, life and goodness, death and evil.

Deuteronomy 30:15

The word *"HaYom"* is famously understood to be an allusion to Rosh Hashanah[1] - the day that humans were first formed and the birthday of the world where again it is held responsible for its actions. This is also true for "the day" that a Jewish boy is held accountable for his actions as a man. Psalms 2:7, the thirteenth verse in the book, is referencing this day of a Bar Mitzvah:[2] אֲסַפְּרָה אֶל־חֹק ה' יְלַדְתִּיךָ: אָמַר אֵלַי בְּנִי אַתָּה אֲנִי הַיּוֹם - I declare, as an

---

[1] Zohar 3:231a.
[2] Lev Simcha.

obligation, that God said to me, My son I birthed you
today.

An immediate consequence of reaching Jewish adulthood
is that one can make new contributions to the spiritual
collective.[3] The *medresh*[4] cites the Prophet Isaiah[5]" עַם־זוּ
יָצַרְתִּי - this nation I formed" as a nod to the shift from
just being a person to being part of a people. "זוּ - *Zu*", the
Rabbis point out, also has a numerical value of thirteen.
These thirteen years also correspond to the Thirteen
Attributes of Mercy.[6] The joy of this day is deeply
connected to the power of the covenant of peoplehood
י"ג מדו"ת ש"ל רחמי"ם = שמח"ת ב"ר מצו"ה (the joy of the
Bar Mitzvah = Thirteen Attributes of Mercy), both
equalling 1091.

Being obligated in commandments is the Divine
expectation of accountability for others. Mitzvah is a
language of connectivity and attachment. Saying the *Shema*
and accepting the yoke of heaven is the first Biblical
Mitzvah that one is commanded as an adult, and is why it
is the subject of the first Mishna in the Talmud.[7] It also
opens with the instruction to cleave to the oneness (אחד)
of God through love (אהבה); both which have a numerical
value of thirteen.

---

[3] See Zohar 2:98a.
[4] Quoted by the Midrash Shmuel.
[5] 43:21.
[6] Emunas Aticha. תשנ"ד.
[7] Chidushie HaRim.

This day marks the beginning of the journey, not its completion. Each and every day consists of choices; actions and inactions. Those decisions, to various degrees, bring us closer or further away from our ultimate goal of a perfected and intimate relationship with the Source of All Good. We all want to choose life, but we don't always realize that the path to get there is paved, in fact, with good deeds.[8]

The Talmud[9] tells the story of the great Rabbi Alexandri who would, like a merchant selling their wares, declare in the street: "מאן בעי חיי מאן בעי חיי" - Who wants life? Who wants life?" Folks would gather around shouting " הב לן חיי" - Give us life!" to which the Rabbi responded[10] " מי האיש החפץ חיים ... Who is the person who desires life סוּר מֵרָע וַעֲשֵׂה־טוֹב בַּקֵּשׁ שָׁלוֹם וְרָדְפֵהוּ... Remove yourself from evil and do good, desire peace and pursue it". It is accessible to everyone but we must want it. As King David wrote[11] גְּדֹלִים מַעֲשֵׂי ה' דְּרוּשִׁים לְכָל־חֶפְצֵיהֶם, "Great are the deeds of God, available to all who want them".[12]

One way to achieve clarity of direction is to see the benefits that come from the good choices we make. King Solomon wrote[13] about the Torah's teachings, "My son . . . they will be life to your soul and a graceful [ornament] for your neck". The Malbim understands this guarantee to be

---

[8] See Rashi 30:15.
[9] Bavli Avoda Zarah 19b.
[10] Psalms 34:13-15.
[11] Psalms 111:2.
[12] See Yismach Moshe for an alternative explanation.
[13] Proverbs 3:21-22.

manifested during the study of Torah, in that grace is generated in the pleasantness of the experience both among people, and God. This is also found in the teaching[14] from Rabbi Chanina ben Dosa who posits that "one with whom people are pleased (chein), God is pleased. But anyone from whom people are displeased, God is displeased.

It is much easier to prepare for a particular day, than it is to show up and be present every day. Rosh HaShanah is one day but it sets the tone for the whole year. A boy's Bar Mitzvah celebration is significant, in that it projects an image of the kind of life he chooses to live. It can be difficult to sustain one's vision across the long experience of time. Finding the sweetness and blessing in the work makes it sustainable.

The Sifrei[15] compares the learning of Torah to the presence of טל Tal-dew: just as the whole world rejoices with dew, so too with the Torah. This can be achieved in seeing the value of the choices we make day in and day out. The word ביום - with the day, equals חן - grace[16]. Seeing ourselves as truly a bar mitzvah, a master of our holy destiny, empowers us to choose the good life - through a life of good deeds.

---

[14] Avos 3:10.
[15] Devarim 306:17.
[16] Rabbi Chaim Elazer of Munkatch.

Vayelech - Graceful Perspective

וַיֹּאמֶר יְהוָה אֶל-מֹשֶׁה, הֵן קָרְבוּ יָמֶיךָ לָמוּת קְרָא אֶת יְהוֹשֻׁעַ
וְהִתְיַצְּבוּ בְּאֹהֶל מוֹעֵד, וַאֲצַוֶּנּוּ; וַיֵּלֶךְ מֹשֶׁה וִיהוֹשֻׁעַ, וַיִּתְיַצְּבוּ
בְּאֹהֶל מוֹעֵד.

Hashem spoke to Moses, "Behold, your days are drawing
near to die; summon Joshua and both of you shall stand in
the Tent of Meeting and I shall command him."

Deuteronomy 31:14

This world is filled with beauty and opportunities for
pleasure. Knowing that our time here won't last forever
can help enhance our appreciation of that goodness. It can
also assist in discerning what is truly good for us. A
grandson[1] of the Bal Shem Tov expounds on the proverb[2]
"grace is a lie, beauty is vanity" - שֶׁקֶר הַחֵן וְהֶבֶל הַיֹּפִי

---

[1] Rabbi Baruch of Mezhibuz (1753-1811).
[2] 31:30.

observing - השקר יש לו חן - that many find grace in the lies of the world and beauty in its vanity.

Moshe was not one of those people. The Medresh teaches that the end of the verse in Proverbs[3] "A woman who fears God is praiseworthy" is actually referring to Moshe.[4] On the day of Moshe's death, he wasn't distracted or enticed by the empty pleasures of this world, instead he was singularly focused on his own spiritual responsibilities; and so he went to the study hall.[5]

The trajectory of Moses' career, from the burning bush to the day of his death, is connected in the Medresh[6] by the word "הן". When God first speaks to Moses and sends him to inform Pharaoh and the Israelites that the time of liberation has come, Moses responds[7] "וְהֵן לֹא־יַאֲמִינוּ לִי - But they will not believe me." Later, Moshe attempts to reclaim the word in praising God[8] הֵן לַיהוָה אֱלֹהֶיךָ הַשָּׁמַיִם וּשְׁמֵי הַשָּׁמָיִם - But to Hashem your God are the heavens and the highest heavens".

According to the Mederesh[9] each letter in the Hebrew Alphabet is partnered with a different letter to achieved the wholeness of its set: ג"ז ב"ח א"ט.[10] This continues with

---

[3] The word "החן" stands for *challah, nida,* and *hadlakas neiros.*
[4] Yalkut Yisro 271.
[5] Targum Yonasan 31:1.
[6] Devarim Rabbah 9:6.
[7] Exodus 4:1.
[8] Deuteronomy 10:14.
[9] Shemos Rabbah 15:7.
[10] 1+9, 2+8, 3+7.

ל"ע כ"פ י"צ.[11] The two letters that do not have a match are the ה and the נ,[12] because they are exactly half of 10 and 100.[13]

When Biliam comes to bless the Jewish People he says about them: "עָם לְבָדָד הֶן - they are a singular people". The Alshich explains that just as the ה and the נ are unique, so too the Jewish people, as a nation, are one of a kind. Perhaps this is what God is saying to Moshe; you, and the way you live your life, are unique and praiseworthy.[14]

Moshe knew more Torah than anyone else, yet he was the humblest of all people,[15] When our gifts are oriented towards God, particularly when they have the potential to be misused, they are elevated and praiseworthy - even the gifts of beauty and grace. The Talmud[16] cautions us:

אָמַר רַב חִיָּיא בַּר אָשִׁי אָמַר רַב תַּלְמִיד חָכָם
צָרִיךְ שֶׁיְהֵא בּוֹ אֶחָד מִשְׁמוֹנָה בִּשְׁמִינִית

Rav Ḥiyya bar Ashi says Rav says: a Torah scholar must have one-eighth of one-eighth [of arrogance - גס].[17]

---

[11] 10+90, 20+80, 30+70.
[12] 5 and 50.
[13] See Rashi Bavli Sukkah 52b for ש ר ק.
[14] "He went" - הלך - has a numerical value of 55.
[15] Numbers 12:3.
[16] Bavli Sotah 5a.
[17] Rashi.

The quality of **גס**, or arrogance, is so pernicious that the the letter "**ס**" never follows a "**ג**", in the entire Torah.[18] The word "**גס**" has a numerical value of 63, alluding to an even smaller, but one less than the 1/64 that is required by the Talmud.[19] One way to understand[20] the unique phrase of "an eighth of an eighth" is to see it as an allusion to the eighth repetition of the eighth letter in Psalm 119.[21] The 64th verse is:

חַסְדְּךָ יְקוָק מָלְאָה הָאָרֶץ
חֻקֶּיךָ לַמְּדֵנִי

> Your kindness, O LORD,
> fills the earth; teach me Your
> laws".

When we see God as filling up the whole world, we are then positioned to learn Torah properly.

The Gra offers a similar interpretation and reads the Talmud as instructing us to look at the eighth verse in the eighth parsha; Vayishlach. The verse[22] reads: קָטֹנְתִּי מִכֹּל הַחֲסָדִים וּמִכָּל־הָאֱמֶת אֲשֶׁר עָשִׂיתָ - I am small because of all of the kindness and truth that you have done.

---

[18] Sefer HaChaim (less in that 63 is less than 64).
[19] Pardes Yosef.
[20] See L'kutie Shoshanim HaShalem.
[21] The first eight begin with א and then the next eight start with ב.
[22] Genesis 32:11.

In moments of arrogance, we distort the reality of our existence by taking up space and credit that doesn't belong to us. This prevents a healthy coexistence with God.[23] We are meant to learn from Moshe, whose awareness of the greatness of God filtered out artificial distractions, such that he is able to remain focused on God until his last breath. Like Moses, we should strive to utilize and enhance our unique talents in graceful partnership with their Source.

---

[23] Bavli Sota 5a.

Haazinu - Graceful Listening

הַאֲזִינוּ הַשָּׁמַיִם, וַאֲדַבֵּרָה; וְתִשְׁמַע הָאָרֶץ, אִמְרֵי-פִי.

Give ear, O heavens, and I will speak; and may the earth hear the words of my mouth.

Deuteronomy 32:1

At the start of the parsha, Moses calls upon Heaven and Earth to listen to his song warning[1] Israel of the consequences of sin. Moses uses "hearing" as a language of understanding, deploying heaven and earth to bear witness to the good intention, and outcome, that God has in identifying the work that still needs to be done in repairing the world.[2]

Moses specifically asks the Heavens to listen before he speaks. The Ahavas Shalom notes that those who have a pious, heavenly way of being, will always listen before

---

[1] Rashi.
[2] Meyer Yenie Chachamim.

speaking. In their minds they will hear what they are about to say, gauge its impact and modify their words when appropriate, before uttering a sound. By contrast, the Ahavas Shalom adds, one who has a more earthly demeanor, will at best only hear their words as they are saying them. This dichotomy echoes the heavenly voice, alluded to in this verse when parsed "the heavens hear, and then speak", as opposed to the more earth based approach of first "hearing the words as the mouth utters them".[3]

Indeed, this mirrors the order of creation[4]: "In the beginning of God/Elokim creating the heaven and earth".[5] However, in the second chapter of Genesis it is reversed: "on the day of God's/Hashem's, making of earth and heaven".[6] The Ohr Hachaim explains the pairing of God's name "Elokim" as being appropriately joined with the pure attribute of judgment in heaven, while on earth there is a partnering with the less strict attribute of mercy, which is manifested through God's ineffable name represented by "Hashem", "The Name".

Just like the original human, Adam, we are also created from both heaven and earth and find ourselves in a constant struggle to increase the soul's influence over the body. In a fascinating exchange[7] between Rebbe Yehudah

---

[3] Ahavas Shalom.
[4] See Yetiv Lev.
[5] Genesis 1:1.
[6] Genesis 2:4.
[7] Bavli Sanhedrin 91b.

HaNasi and Antoninos, Rebbe interprets the verse: "God calls to the heavens above and to the earth that God may judge God's people" as: "heaven - this is the soul, earth - this is the body". "השמים - the heavens" has the same numerical value as "נשמה - soul" because it comes from heaven.[8]

The Ahavas Shalom compares the "we will do and we will listen - נעשה ונשמע" to the relationship between the six days of the work week and the Shabbat. He argues that just as hearing is an act of receiving, so too the Shabbat is given to us for our souls to receive. He connects it to the verse: "יִשְׂמְחוּ הַשָּׁמַיִם וְתָגֵל הָאָרֶץ - Let the heavens rejoice and the earth exult" as the influence of the spiritual on the physical which results from the work of refining our sensitivities to the Divine, and then subsequently to be guided and exalted by them.

He further observes God's name, alluded to in the first letters of the four words in the verse when spelled out - יו"ד ה"י וא"ו ה"ה - have the same numerical value as the word for "ear - אזן- ozen" and the root of this week's portion "Hazenu". The medresh[9] uses this as the source that heaven has an ear and continues to cite two additional verses to support the claim that heaven also has a heart and a mouth. The first letter of these three words[10] אזן לב פה form the word אלף aleph, the first letter of the Hebrew

---

[8] Pesach Einayim.
[9] Devorim Rabbah 10:4.
[10] "Ear, heart, mouth".

Alphabet, and speak to the need of repairing the world, from the very beginning.

The Vilna Gaon[11] explains the verse "We will do and we will listen" as corresponding to two different aspects of our being. "We will do" refers to the commandments that are unique to the body, while "We will listen" correlates to the learning of Torah and things designated for the soul and intellect as well. He argues it is for that reason that Moses starts with addressing the soul's comprehension before the earthy body.

It is often difficult to hear about one's own shortcomings or failures. However, when we heed God's charge of elevating the physical world to one of spirituality and take responsibility for our choices because it is the right thing to do - when we can really feel that it is the right thing to do - it makes it a lot easier to make the right choice.

This also obtains in conversations with people. We speak to folks because we want them to hear what we have to say. The Talmud[12] teaches that whoever has an awareness of God's awesomeness, their words are listened to. It is the presence of חן, grace, that facilitates the success of this type of speech.[13] The words "grace" and "ear" " אזן - חן" both share the numerical value of 58, as well as God's name mentioned above[14].

---

[11] See Aderes Eleyahu for many additional insights on this verse.
[12] Bavli Brachos 6b see also Ben Yehoyada.
[13] Ahavas Shalom.
[14] Shem Havaya spelled out.

The verse of האזינו asks us to continually listen to the heavenly words of the Torah and allow them to penetrate into our heart and arouse our soul. When we do so, the words that we speak will invariably be filled with grace and will in turn be easier for others to hear.

Vezos Habracha - Graceful Living

וַיָּמָת שָׁם מֹשֶׁה עֶבֶד־יְקוֶק בְּאֶרֶץ מוֹאָב עַל־פִּי יהוה.

And Moses, servant of Hashem, died there, in the land of Moab, by the mouth of Hashem.

Deuteronomy 34:5

Humanity comes into being with a breath from the Divine. The Torah begins the story of our interaction with a moment of intimacy between God and Adam, and concludes its final verses of Deuteronomy with Mose's death through a Divine kiss. These two events are deeply connected and an aspect of the relationship is alluded to in the verse[1]

וַיִּפַּח בְּאַפָּיו נִשְׁמַת חַיִּים וַיְהִי הָאָדָם
לְנֶפֶשׁ חַיָּה

---

[1] Genesis 2:7.

"and God breathed into his
nostrils the soul of life; and Adam
became a living soul".

In the Hebrew, the last letter of each word forms the
phrase: "and Mose died" - , another way of וימת משה[2]
connecting the beginning and the end of the Torah.

In Sefer Yetzirah[3], the letter "ת" governs "חן" - grace, and
corresponds to the "פה בנפש" - the mouth in the soul.
The mouth is so powerful that King Solomon writes[4]
"Death and Life are in the power of the tongue - מָוֶת
וְחַיִּים בְּיַד־לָשׁוֹן". The letter "ת" has a numerical value of
400, as do the words "יד לשון" - the power of the tongue.
When a person misuses this power and speaks badly of
another, literally a bad tongue, they are punished with the
affliction of being a *metzora,* often translated as leprosy.[5]
Metzora - מצרע also has a numerical value of 400[6] and such
a person is considered dead,[7] until they go through the
atonement process.

The Talmud[8] further elaborates on the binary potential of
the final letter of the Hebrew alphabet, the "ת": Rav said "
תָּיו" Tuv - will live - will die. "תָּיו" - תִּחְיֶה, "תָּיו" - תָּמוּת
However, even life and death turn out to not be a binary.

---

[2] Agra DeKala Genesis.
[3] 4:14.
[4] Proverbs 18:21.
[5] Midrash Tanchuma Metzora 2.
[6] Chamra Tava.
[7] Bavli Nedarim 64b.
[8] Bavli Shabbos 55a.

For example, wicked people are called "dead" while they are still alive, while the righteous are called alive even after their souls are returned to their source.[9] There is even a position in the Talmud[10] that Moses never died.[11]

Moses is described as dying שם, there. The Talmud, using the exegetical principle of a *gezerah shavah*, connects the moment of Moses' death to the moment when Moses received the Ten Commandments: "וְאֶתְּנָ֨ה לְךָ֜ וֶהְיֵה־שָׁ֗ם אֶת־לֻחֹ֤ת הָאֶ֙בֶן֙ וְהַתּוֹרָה֙ וְהַמִּצְוָ֔ה אֲשֶׁ֥ר כָּתַ֖בְתִּי לְהוֹרֹתָֽם - wait there, and I will give you the stone tablets with the teachings and commandments which I have inscribed to instruct them".[12] The Talmud continues: "Just as there, he was standing and serving [before God]; so too, here" after his death.

Rav Meir Simcha of Dvinsk[13] explains that it is angels who stand in a particular spiritual place, while people have the unique ability to grow and transcend their current location. It is this constant striving for greater perfection that gives us spiritual mobility. King David describes it[14] as "My feet are on a straight path. In assemblies I will bless God". The mystics[15] understand this to be a reference to תיקון זה סוד התי"ו - the redeeming of the letter "tuv", that without the

---

[9] Bavli Berachos 18a-b.
[10] Bavli Sotah 13b.
[11] See also the Satmar Rebbe.
[12] Exodus 24:12.
[13] Meshach Chachma.
[14] Psalms 26:12.
[15] Derech Etz Chaim (Ramchal).

"foot" at the bottom left, advancing the cause, it would be the letter "ח".

This also speaks to the positive impact that we all want to have in this world. The world shouldn't, and can't, be the same without us. Our ability to make a difference isn't limited just to the time we are alive. The Rabbis teach: גדולים צדיקים במיתתן יותר מבחייהן the righteous are even greater after their passing than while they are living.[16]

Perhaps this is why the order of King's Solomon's teaching places life after death: "Death and life are in the power of speech".[17] This follows the Talmud's[18] assertion:

דאמר רבי יוחנן משום רבי שמעון בן יוחי
כל ת"ח שאומרים דבר שמועה מפיו בעולם
הזה שפתותיו דובבות בקבר

> Rabbi Yochanan said in the name
> of Rabbi Shimon ben Yochai:
> Every scholar whose Torah is
> recited, their lips move in the grave.

It is possible that the Torah is emphasizing our ability to live on through our teachings and good deeds with the placement of this verse, as Moses dies, while eight verses of the Torah remain to be written.

---

[16] Bavli Chullin 7b.
[17] R' S. of Belz .
[18] Bavli Yevamos 97a.

Moshe was worthy of dying through a kiss from God because he sanctified his body as a vessel for Divine service.[19] We are also able to live with a constant intimacy and closeness that offers us the opportunity to partner with the Creator in improving and enhancing this world, and the lives of those in it. As we look forward to reading Genesis next week, we recognize that beginnings and endings are fluid, and that a life lived with grace will always overflow the physical boundaries of time.

---

[19] R' Moshe Dovid Veli.

Festivals

Our Father, Our King: Divine Masculinity on Rosh Hashanah[1]

Speaking about masculinity today, in a favorable way, is so tricky that it is often easier not to discuss it. On Rosh Hashanah however, when so much masculine God language is deployed, it's impossible to ignore it. God is a father, a king, a stern and exacting male judge. Our reluctance to discuss positive or graceful masculinity only contributes to the paucity of proper role models. Perhaps our discomfort with the language can be channeled into a form of repentance by assiduously exploring the ways that God models appropriate masculinity.

---

[1] Co-authored with Rabba Wendy Amsellem for HBI on September 26, 2019.

The first truth that men must accept, before they can learn any positive masculinity from God, is that they, themselves, are not gods. God is rightfully at the center of the world, but men have traditionally concluded, in error, that the world revolves around them. God sits in judgment of humans but it is not our place to judge others. Getting past this absurd arrogance is a precondition to being able to learn how God's interactions with people can serve as a productive model.

The Talmud in Tractate Sotah relates that Rabbi Chama b'Rabbi Chanina said: "You shall walk after the Lord your God";[2] but is it possible for a person to walk after the Divine Presence? Is it not written, "For the Lord your God is a consuming fire?" Rather follow the attributes of God, God clothes the naked, visits the sick, comforts mourners, and buries the dead."

God demonstrates a caring and compassionate way of interacting with the world and we are meant to learn from those actions. The Petach Anayim, an 18th century mystical work by Chaim Yossi David Azulai (the Chida) reads the verse of "You shall walk after the Lord your God" as teaching that when we emulate the 13 attributes of mercy we must start after the ones which are names of God. By this the Chida means that we should adopt God's merciful behavior without ever daring to think that we might actually be called to occupy the space that is God's alone.

---

[2] Deuteronomy 4:24.

The false promise offered in the garden by the snake on the first Rosh Hashanah was just that: "Eat and then you will be like God".[3] After the sin, eight verses later, we hear: "The serpent deceived me – השיאני". At least then there was clarity of the mistake. The rabbis point out that the Hebrew word used here for deception has the same letters as "יש אני" (there is – I) to teach that the snake tempted us by convincing us that we could be in the place of God. Consequently, we ruined certain dynamics of our relationship with God by not seeing God for who God really is.

In the mystical tradition, through this sin we defiled the letter *daled* – ד, which represents *dalos* – humility in God's names of *Sha-die* שד-י and *Ado-ni* אדנ-י, leaving just *yesh* יש (there is) and *ani* אני (I).

This month of Elul corresponds to the tribe of Gad גד. Their tribal position was at the front line when the nation went to battle. The stone that represented Gad in the High Priest's breastplate was the *achalmah* (amethyst) אחלמה, that was meant to inspire courage to continue advancing the cause. The tribe of Gad גד also represents a unique blend of confidence and humility. The ג by itself, stands for גיאות, arrogant pride, but coupled with the aforementioned ד of modesty, it creates the necessary awareness of human vulnerability to be present as self, but not for self.

---

[3] Genesis 3:5.

Hillel, who the Talmud testifies was exceedingly humble, said it best: "If I am not for myself, who will be for me. But if I am only for myself what am I – אם אין אני לי מי לי." Perhaps this is the intention of Elul as אני לדודי: the "I" must go and belong to God, the true Beloved.

Like the tribe of Gad, we must have the courage to continue the struggle against toxic masculinity. By remembering that all of our actions must be for God (and not in the place of God), we can end the apathy towards the mentality that boys will be boys.

God's forcefulness and strength are emphasized in the high holiday prayers. But God's might is used to protect the vulnerable. God has great emotional range, power, and agency – but we emphasize that God would prefer to forgive than to be angry. God uses God's power to elevate, inspire, and empower others, not to grind them down. We can learn from God's attributes how to be better men and better humans. As we engage this Rosh Hashanah, let us pray for the courage and grace to find a more favorable form of being.

Sukkot: Imagining The Framework For A Better World[1]

This is the week in the Jewish calendar when we shift focus from repentance and introspection into the world of action. We move from the preparations and reflections of Elul, and the fasting and praying on Yom Kippur, to the immediate building of our *sukkot*. We try hard to live up to the ideals of our newly penitent selves and to persevere in the goals we have recently set. One of the best ways to prevent falling into old patterns and habits is to step away from our familiar structures and systems, and to reposition ourselves anew in the *sukkah*.

An important step in creating a better society (and *sukkah*!) is having a clear sense of what we are trying to construct.

---

[1] Co-authored with Rabba Wendy Amsellem for HBI on September 30, 2020

Sometimes it is hard to imagine the possibilities. When I (Wendy) was a student, Justice Ruth Bader Ginsburg told us that during her first year of law school, in 1956, she and the handful of other women in her class were asked by the law school dean to justify taking the place of a man at Harvard Law School. Justice Ginsberg explained that at that point in her life she had not yet fully discovered her feminism and she was fearful of sounding too aggressive. She told the dean that she had come to law school to better understand her husband's career and that maybe one day it would lead to a part-time job. When we heard this story, we were deeply moved that Justice Ginsburg herself could not foresee how her career would develop.

In a 2016 essay in the New York Times, Justice Ginsburg reported that school children visiting the Supreme Court often asked her, "Did you always want to be a judge, or more exorbitantly, a Supreme Court justice?" Ginsburg noted, "To today's youth, judgeship as an aspiration for a girl is not at all outlandish." Things which are hard to imagine today can swiftly become commonplace. Justice Ginsburg taught us that it is important to challenge the assumption that the way things have been is itself a justifiable reason for them to continue that way, even if we are not sure what the replacements will be.

As the people of Israel traveled through the wilderness, they also did not know from day to day where they were going. The Talmud[2] explains that we dwell in *sukkot* to commemorate the "Clouds of Glory/Clouds of Dignity"

---

[2] Bavli Sukkah 11b.

(*ananei hakavod*) that protected the Israelites in the wilderness and directed them on their journey. Bavli Taanit[3] teaches that there were three miracles that God performed for the people of Israel in the desert. God provided the people with water, *manna*, and clouds of glory. Our rabbis ask why it is only the cloud that merited having a festival or scriptural commandment to remember it?

Rabbi Chaim Yosef David Azulai[4] explains that the clouds of glory are evidence of God's special love for us. Food and water are basic necessities, but the clouds of glory provide comfort and honor to people living in a wilderness. Maimonides[5] explains that the laws of the Torah provide mercy, kindness, and peace " רַחֲמִים וְחֶסֶד וְשָׁלוֹם". God's kindness to us in providing clouds of glory is memorialized each year in the commandment to build a sukkah. It is not coincidental that the numerical value of peace (שלום) is the same as the phrase mercy and kindness (רַחֲמִים וְחֶסֶד) because one is dependent on the other. In our evening prayers, we ask that God spread out over us "God's Sukkah of Peace." By creating structures that advance dignity, and not just survival, we help to build God's Sukkah of Peace.

The three gifts that God gave the Israelites in the desert are associated with their three leaders.[6] The water was

---

[3] 9a.
[4] 1724-1806.
[5] Laws of Shabbat 2:3.
[6] Taanit 9a.

provided in the merit of Miriam; the *manna* in the merit of Moshe; and the clouds of glory are in the merit of Aaron. Aaron was a person who valued dignity, peace, and love. According to the rabbis, Aaron was a perennial peacemaker, rushing to settle quarrels and promote affection between spouses, friends, and enemies. We are taught[7] to be disciples of Aaron; love peace, pursue peace, love creations, and bring people closer to the Torah.

The Sukkah then is not only a commemoration of God's love for us, but also of Aaron's values of collegiality and peace. As we remember one of our more contemporary leaders, Justice Ruth Bader Ginsburg z"l, we recall that she too valued collegiality and friendship. Justice Ginsburg had clear and strong ideals but she was famous for cultivating warm friendships with colleagues who held dramatically different opinions about law and society.

Aaron, as the Kohen Gadol, was also instructed to wear garments of honor and dignity, as part of his job description.[8] Aaron used his dignified position not to seek more power for himself, but to pursue peace in the world of action. He was successful in orchestrating resolutions because people felt how deeply he cared about them. Aaron understood that peace, not money or power, was the greatest blessing. The commentators point out that the phrase "good grace" has the same numerical value as "Kohen", 75, because that is the essence of the priestly

---

[7] Avos 1:12.
[8] Exodus 28:2.

role; to extend the Divine Presence to the people, not to hoard or exploit it.

King Solomon wrote in Proverbs,[9] "A good name is preferred to wealth, and good grace (chein) is better than silver and gold (נִבְחָר שֵׁם מֵעֹשֶׁר רָב מִכֶּסֶף וּמִזָּהָב חֵן טוֹב:). Proverbs reminds us that what we may see as our "permanent" acquisitions are really external to who we are and often quite temporary. There is a false grace that is superficial and fleeting, but the good grace is empowering and instills a sense of responsibility for the greater good to prevent injustice. The first letter of the first four words of the verse which spell "נשמר – to guard" allude to this.

The Talmud[10] tells us that we must leave our permanent houses and move into temporary homes. But later,[11] advises us that for the seven days of *Sukkot* we should make our *sukkot* into our permanent houses. One way to understand this apparent contradiction is that we must look at socially constructed privileges as temporary and external, and utilize the time in the *sukkah* to remember that we were dehumanized in Egypt and God reminded us of our worth. The festival of *Sukkot* is a time to plan for a better model that prioritizes human dignity as essential. Then, we can then make the temporary permanent by disrupting the systems that perpetuate injustice and

---

[9] 22:1.
[10] Bavli Sukkah 2a.
[11] Bavli Sukkah 28b.

protections for the entitled at the expense of those who are truly afflicted.

The struggle to take our resources and use them for the greater good is observed by the Talmud[12] through the order of the Hebrew alphabet. "If we do acts of loving kindness to those in need (*gimmel* and *daled*) then God (*heh* and *vav*) will sustain (*zein*) and provide good grace (*chet tet*). The rabbis point out that if we misuse those resources selfishly then it is the root of evil and sin (*cheit* 'חט').

Building a more just and equitable society is complicated, difficult work. It requires us to re-examine fundamental assumptions about how our communities work and to be willing to dismantle structures of injustice. The way forward is not always clear, but as we build our *sukkot* we can begin to imagine setting up the framework of a better world. In his eulogy, Chief Justice John Roberts remembered, "Ruth used to ask, 'What is the difference between a bookkeeper in Brooklyn and a Supreme Court Justice?' She would answer: 'One generation.'" Our actions, to continue the struggle for equality and dignity for all, will make what comes next possible.

May the memory of Ruth Bader Ginsburg be a blessing in that it motivates us to be agents of graceful change.

---

[12] Shabbat 104a.

Purim - Esther and the Pursuit of Likeability[1]

In this election season, there has been a focus on whether candidates, especially female candidates, are sufficiently likeable. Likeability is a virtue as it indicates whether a candidate is attuned to others and can get them on board to work with them. Likeability can even be translated as חן, an ability to be found gracious by others.

Esther, a heroine of the holiday of Purim, is the queen of likeability. In Chapter 2 of the Book of Esther, Esther is described as נשאת חן בעיני כל רואיה, she is found graceful by all who see her. At first this seems like an ideal situation – Esther is liked by everyone! Yet, it is also kind of odd. Is it really possible to be liked by all people?

[1]Co-authored with Rabba Wendy Amsellem for HBI on March 9, 2020.

Rabbi Elazar, in the Talmud,[2] explains that Esther appeared to each and every person as if she was a member of their nationality. To the Persians, she appeared Persian. To the Medeans, she appeared Medean. They did not see Esther for who she actually was. Instead she became, in their eyes, whomever they wanted her to be.

Rabbi Yuda, in the *midrash*,[3] takes this a step further. He explains that Esther was like a statue whom a thousand people can equally admire. In his understanding, Esther did not present as a distinctive personality with independent thoughts, opinions and predilections. Instead she was a blank canvas of a person upon whom others projected their idealized desires.

This is a familiar trap for women. In order to have חן, to move about the world in a state of grace, women are told to be everything to everyone, to blunt the more distinctive aspects of themselves in order to be likeable.

For Esther, this comes at the cost of an expression of selfhood. As long as Esther is a statue, everyone can like her. Esther is afraid that if she gives voice to her own ideas, she will sacrifice her likability. And so the real Esther, as her name implies, remains hidden.

Esther's pliability and willingness to be whomever others want her to be reaches grotesque expression in the continuation of the passage in Bavli Megillah.[4] The

---

[2] Bavli Megillah 13a.
[3] Esther Rabbah 6:9.
[4] 13a.

Talmud cites Esther[5] "The King loved Esther more than all of the other women and she found favor in his eyes more than all of the other virgins". Rav explains that Esther is favored above all the women and all the virgins because her body can transform into whatever the King desires. If he wanted the feeling of intercourse with a virgin, Esther could provide that. If he wanted the feeling of being with a sexually experienced woman, Esther could provide that as well. She is the King's fantasy, mutable according to his desires.

This is not true חן. חן is not about scooping yourself out so that you become only a reflection of what others want. חן is about expressing yourself in a way that is cognizant of those around you, while still maintaining your personhood, in relationship with God.

Proverbs[6] warns שקר החן והבל היופי, sometimes grace is false and beauty meaningless. חן is not an end in itself. חן that is only fixated on how others see you is שקר, falsehood. It is easy to get caught up in the desire to be well liked. The Ishbitzer Rebbe, in Mei HaShiloach, writes that "Find favor in the eyes of God and people"[7] is followed by "Trust in God with all your heart and do not rely on your own wisdom". The Ishbitzer teaches that these verse are juxtaposed because if people are unduly preoccupied with finding favor in the eyes of others, they should focus their intentions on God, and fulfilling God's

---

[5] 2:17.
[6] 31:30.
[7] Proverbs 3:4.

will, and in this way they can achieve חן in the eyes of both God and people.

Indeed, this is what Esther does. When she realizes that God wants her to save God's people, she is able to find the courage to express her distinctive self. Esther stands before the King as an out Jewish woman and makes a powerful argument to save her people. She asks for something real and important and the King can see her for who she actually is and finds her full of grace.

The story of the book of Esther is how Esther goes from the false חן of Chapter 2 to the true חן of Chapter 7. She stops trying to obey and please everyone and in doing so she finds her voice and her power. Purim celebrates the process of revealing the hidden truth and giving it expression to the outside world. As we read the Book of Esther may we be inspired to find true חן in the eyes of God and people, and the strength to persist in doing God's work.

Shavuot In A Heightened State Of Grace[1]

Chein is sometimes hard to describe but we know it when
we see it. It is that extra measure of grace that makes a
person or an action especially appealing. *Chein* elevates the
ordinary, exceeds our expectations, and inspires us to be
more graceful as well.

It is perhaps because grace transcends the natural
limitations that it is so difficult to articulate and achieve. In
our tradition, the number seven represents the spectrum of
the natural order and the cycle of the seven days of
creation. From Passover to Shavuot, we count seven
weeks, for a total of 49 days. This number seven,
multiplied by itself, represents the greatest expression of
the essence of nature. But it is only on the next day, the

---

[1] Co-authored with Rabba Wendy Amsellem for HBI on May
26, 2020

50th that goes beyond these boundaries, that we are able to receive the Torah.

Like the relationship between our body and soul, the Torah is where the finite meets the infinite. *Chein* is spelled in Hebrew חן – the numerical value of ן = 50 and ח = 8. Both the number 50 and the number 8 exceed the regular natural order which is based on factors of 7. *Chein* is above nature.

Megilat Ruth is replete with acts of *chein* that break natural assumptions. Ruth and Orpah, the Moabite daughters-in-law of Naomi, escort her on her way back to Bethlehem. Naomi explains that there is no future for the young women there and urges them to return to their parents' homes in Moab. The word Moab itself has the Hebrew numerical value of 49, indicating that returning there would be the natural thing to do. Orpah makes the reasonable choice to turn back, but Ruth clings to Naomi fiercely, pledging her unswerving loyalty.

Ruth goes beyond what is expected of her, choosing not only Naomi's company but also her God, her people, and her way of life. In truth, all Jews who are converts do this – they break from the assumed rhythms of their lives and embark instead on an extraordinary path of spiritual expansion.

We read Megilat Ruth on *Shavuot* because *Shavuot* is about going beyond the letter of the law. On *Shavuot*, the people of Israel break with their previous patterns of behavior and perform the ultimate elevating act of accepting the Torah. In doing so, they model the *kabbalat mitzvot*, accepting of commandments, that is traditionally the most essential part of the conversion process.

Boaz also exceeds expectations. As a field owner, he is obligated in the mitzvah of *leket*, allowing the poor to pick up sheaves dropped by his gleaners. Boaz not only performs the basic mitzvah of *leket*, but he instructs his workers to drop extra sheaves[2] so that Ruth can collect them. He takes notice of Ruth, a defenseless stranger, and he speaks kindly to her. Ruth responds to him by asking, "Why have I found *chein* in your eyes, even though I am a stranger?"[3] Boaz explains that he has heard of her devotion to Naomi and then he blesses Ruth. She responds, "May I find *chein* in your eyes sir because you have comforted me and spoken to my heart."[4]

Ruth understands Boaz's behavior to be motivated by *chein*. He is showing her kindness above and beyond expectation. Boaz replies that his acts of chen are directly in response to Ruth's extraordinary behavior.

Boaz uses Abraham-like language to describe Ruth, saying to her, "It has been told to me. . . how you left your father, your mother, and the land of your birth to go to a nation that you did not know."[5] Abraham is the first and most potent example of a person leaving their expected life to go forth on a spiritual journey. By veering from the norm, Abraham is the model for all of his spiritual descendents,

---

[2] Ruth 2:16.
[3] Ruth 2:10.
[4] Ruth 2:13.
[5] Ruth 2:11.

converts who leave their former lives to follow the God of Abraham. As Maimonides says in his letter to Ovadiah the Convert, "Whoever converts . . .is counted among the disciples of Abraham our father."

How does a person make these choices and acquire this state of grace? The Gra explains that *chein* comes from the language of *chenam* (free). One cannot buy *chein*. Rather it, like the Torah, is a gift from God, for those who choose to exert themselves. By giving freely of ourselves to others and offering more than is expected of us, we emulate God and are imbued with Divine grace.

The Midrash Tanchuma, a collection of early rabbinic homiletic teachings, observes that in the Book of Ruth, except for eight verses, every verse begins with the Hebrew letter vav. These eight non-vav verses highlight Ruth's connection to the number eight and her journey to the supernatural. She goes above and beyond the physical, for the sake of the spiritual. Even her name רות, with a numerical value of 606, alludes to this. Ruth chooses to add 606 additional commandments to the basic seven Noahide laws, (the seven commandments given to Noah and his descendants), so that in the end she accepts the 613 commandments of the Torah.

Men are often taught that to be responsible one must respectfully follow the rules, but in truth, it is not nearly enough. Systems are maintained by people continuing to do what people have done and expected in the past. Societal constructions of gender and their roles perpetuate assumptions as norms that actually limit and distort our true purpose and potential. We must expect more if things are ever going to improve.

It is especially challenging to strive for *chein* because it feels amorphous. Every year *Shavuot* invites us to re-experience the beyond. By adopting a stance of generosity and pushing above standard expectations, we can all experience, and emerge from, Shavuot in a heightened state of grace.

Made in the USA
Middletown, DE
12 December 2021